Taoism in Act[ion]

Do not think of self. . . . In the Tao, parents think of their children first. Single mother Mapita Sanchez discusses the choices she made at home and on the job that allowed her to make her twin sons her number one priority.

The material is fleeting; the spiritual is everlasting. . . . The Tao recognizes that good parenting is not dependent on materialistic values. Dot and John Singleton's blended family includes three girls and two boys from previous marriages. In these pages, they describe their family night that made togetherness more valuable than name brand clothes or video games.

Discipline yourself before trying to discipline others. . . . The Tao says teaching by example is the best lesson. Lew and Margaret Williams, who don't always agree on parenting techniques, wanted their children to love reading, so they read to them daily . . . and carefully monitored television viewing for all family members, not just the kids.

Follow the middle road; it is the heart of knowing. . . . Balancing the elements of various philosophies and lifestyles is part of the Way for wise parents. Carl and Kate Flanagan, who hail from different cultural and ethnic backgrounds, explain: "When it comes to rules, you can't have too many absolutes. There are always adjustments to be made for each child and set of circumstances."

Sample these valuable lessons . . . and more from . . .

The Tao of Parenting

Greta Nagel, Ph.D., author of *The Tao of Teaching*, received her doctorate in education from San Diego State University and The Claremont Graduate School. She was an elementary and high school teacher for fifteen years and an elementary school principal for eight years before taking a teaching position at California State Polytechnic University. Dr. Nagel also studied Eastern Religion at the School of Theology at Claremont College. She lives with her family in Fullerton, California.

ALSO BY GRETA NAGEL

The Tao of Teaching

THE TAO
OF
PARENTING

The Ageless Wisdom
of Taoism and the
Art of Raising Children

GRETA NAGEL, Ph.D.

A PLUME BOOK

PLUME
Published by the Penguin Group
Penguin Putnam Inc., 375 Hudson Street, New York, New York 10014, U.S.A.
Penguin Books Ltd, 27 Wrights Lane, London W8 5TZ, England
Penguin Books Australia Ltd, Ringwood, Victoria, Australia
Penguin Books Canada Ltd, 10 Alcorn Avenue, Toronto, Ontario, Canada M4V 3B2
Penguin Books (N.Z.) Ltd, 182–190 Wairau Road, Auckland 10, New Zealand

Penguin Books Ltd, Registered Offices: Harmondsworth, Middlesex, England

First published by Plume, an imprint of Dutton NAL,
a member of Penguin Putnam Inc.

First Printing, November, 1998
10 9 8 7 6 5 4 3

Ⓟ REGISTERED TRADEMARK—MARCA REGISTRADA

LIBRARY OF CONGRESS CATALOGING-IN-PUBLICATION DATA:

Nagel, Greta.
The Tao of parenting : the ageless wisdom of Taoism and the art of raising
children / Greta Nagel.
p. cm.
ISBN 0-452-28005-2
1. Child rearing.   2. Parenting.   3. Tao.   I. Title.
HQ769.N196   1998
649'.1—dc21   98-19436
                                                           CIP

Printed in the United States of America
Set in Sabon
Designed by Julian Hamer

To my family,
all of you,
with gratitude forever
for
your love,
your support,
and the many things
you have taught me.

Acknowledgments

Thanks, first of all, to my participant families. Their patience with my questions and their many hours of gracious hospitality will never be forgotten. Although their identities herein are pseudonyms, they have become more real to me as human beings than ever. For their many kindnesses and wonderful insights, I will be grateful always.

I will always appreciate Art Fleming for encouraging me to write this book. He and his wife Rita have been true friends as I have learned to navigate the strange waters of writing for publication. In memoriam I wish to thank Donald I. Fine for his kind and encouraging words.

For their professional and friendly insights I am indebted to Carol Weinstein, Betty Thompson, and Sylvia Maxson. They helped me come to see that this book serves an important need. For their support and encouragement, I shall always remember my sister, Joy Anderson, and my friend Irma Jayaweera. They told me I was a writer. Thanks to Pat Irot, Dixie Shaw, Peggy Hammer, Judy Sowell, Connie Bannon, Donna Padgett, Jean Marie Sohlden Fisher, and Polly Gast for their excitement and enthusiasm. Thanks to Pat Wegner, Gordon Nielsen, and Maria Linder Nielsen, as well as to Darlene Sellers, Terry Kristiansen, Fred and Ellen Lentz, and Sharon Jackson for their support. They helped me to believe in myself. And for their assistance in preparing stages of the manuscript as well as for their insights and encouragement, I am grateful to Janet Vest, Christina Nagel, Paul Nagel, and my talented editor, Jennifer Moore.

And to Glenn, I can't say thank you enough for your patience, your encouragement, and your willingness to let other things go. Imagine, no tuna casserole for many months.

Contents

Introduction

I imagine that when you picked up this book, you wondered if it might help you, or someone close to you, to be a better parent. As I talk to parents from many different communities, I learn that they are all very concerned about guiding their children in these challenging times. Every week, we read disturbing news about other people's children around us. We all wonder what influences will affect our own offspring.

Sometimes, just when we think our own families are "home free" in this process of child raising, our offspring portray traits that were never part of the plan. We are reminded that traveling life's roads means taking curves and making turns. We also see how our children are, indeed, our children for the rest of our lives, and we are their parents for the rest of theirs. Most of us knew it wouldn't be easy. We just didn't want it to be so difficult.

Futurists and others who study our changing world tell us that changes of all sorts are occurring more and more rapidly as time progresses. Advances in technology that once took thousands, then hundreds, of years to occur are now happening within only a few years. Misunderstandings between generations are occurring at a more rapid rate as well. Parents have always been surprised by the generation gaps that occur with each new decade. Now, the cultural distances between parents and children can grow greater in even shorter amounts of time. A word like *dope* can take on new meaning every four years. Moms and dads find themselves sorting through a new maze of styles in dress, music, sexuality, and the use of addictive substances.

The quality of the current gap is affected by a world where popular movies feature killing frenzies and the names of rock groups sound like drug ads and death threats. Parents often come to feel clueless and powerless. They leap at small chances to connect when styles that they once knew (Bell bottoms! Polyester!) fly back into fashion for a moment in time. They are concerned when their children have dangerous habits, like smoking and drinking, even though they themselves once did the same things. They feel betrayed when activities or styles that they hold in contempt are attractive to their children.

In order to be successful parents, fathers and mothers need to feel empowered with inner strength and outer technique. Perhaps now more than ever, they need to have a wide range of abilities in order to interact effectively with their children. The positive response of readers to my previous book, *The Tao of Teaching*, tells me that people are interested not only in gaining skills but also in forming a sound philosophical ground for their actions.

I hope that this book will help you in your own explorations. You will, perhaps, come to feel that *The Tao of Parenting* is a comfortable friend. With concepts well over two thousand years old, its perspectives aren't new, but it may renew long-held beliefs for you. It will remind you that strength comes from being calm and that it is important to pay attention to your children and to the small details of life. It will provide opportunities for you to review the benefits of listening and the joys of being tender. It will encourage you to reaffirm that growth comes from positive support.

This book is meant to be easy to use. You don't have to read it straight through from front to back. You may find yourself picking it up one evening to read several chapters in the middle and reading a different batch of chapters the next evening. Many people tell me that this flexibility makes it a perfect book for the bedside table. And this book isn't really just for adults; teenagers should find many points to read and discuss here. (I don't, however, advocate that parents hand it over as assigned reading for offspring. That would not be part of the Way.)

The stories that you will read here are about four real families. (Their names have been changed to ensure their privacy.) This book is about how four sets of parents have supported and interacted with their children as they developed into adults—all now in their late teens and twenties. These are not tales of raising perfect children, for as they have grown, many of them have struggled with difficult issues relating to beliefs, behaviors, and identity, and they have confronted the temptations of drugs and sex that permeate today's society. Nor are these narratives of perfect parents, for these parents can identify many mistakes they have made along the way. Nevertheless, these parents have guided their children to adulthood, helping them become capable, caring, and strong.

Perhaps you have already read *The Tao of Teaching*, my first book that applies the Tao; it has eighty-one chapters, since the messages of the ancient *Tao Te Ching* were presented in eighty-one chapters. I have used the same format for this book. Many people have written to me or talked to me about their appreciation for *The Tao of Teaching*, and many of them have also suggested, "Why don't you write a book for parents?" *The Tao of Teaching* was written with parents in mind and was not intended just for classroom teachers, and there are many conceptual similarities between that book and this one, but the stories told here are all family based.

You won't always see the parents in these stories "bringing up" their kids, but their children don't just "grow up" either. There is a great deal of guidance going on, back and forth between and among parents and children. Even if you have not read any other books about the Tao, the ideas here may seem familiar. You will examine parenting virtues (like patience, honesty, modeling, and simplicity) that have been shared by many cultures throughout the history of our world. You will also be reminded of some of the good parenting advice that already abounds in our own daily culture. From Ann Landers or Dear

Abby or Robert Wallace and beyond, the good word is out there and available. We are all trying to help our children become happy, responsible adults.

The Tao is, however, unique in its particular combinations of advice. Books like *The Tao of Physics* and *The Tao of Pooh*, have shown us Westerners how Taoist interpretations can help us better understand how to live. Right off the bat, we learn from the Tao that there are no formulas. What works for one child doesn't always work for another. What works for one family doesn't always work for another. I am reminded of watching one mother, my friend, talking to her daughter before the eleven-year-old went off to a slumber party. Her inquisition was lengthy: "Do you have your pajamas? Do you have your pillow? Do you have your sleeping bag? Do you have your comb? Do you have your toothbrush? Do you have your retainer? Do you have the gift? Do you have your underwear? . . ." I listened with growing discomfort—at first because I felt guilty that I was such an incomplete mom. All I usually ever asked was: "Do you have everything?" My kids would respond yes, and off they would go. Later, I came to see that my responsibility as mother meant not thinking for my children. I never did develop a grand inquisitor style, although I do always ask my son if he's remembered his toothbrush, mostly for effect, just in case he'll feel good that I care. I also care a lot about the financial impact of more cavities!

You will probably notice that this volume is, first of all, a book of philosophy. I want to help parents apply the wisdom of the Tao as we face the millennium. Its concepts, as old as they are, align well with our current interest in appreciating our children and our families and in playing it cool as we go with the flow.

Taoist philosophy stresses the importance of modeling, so this book shows you how several real parents enact Taoist philosophical concepts in their daily lives. The stories you are about to read are true; they are about people I have known and events that have occurred in their four families over the years. Only their names have been changed. I have come to know them all quite well in recent years, but I have been acquainted with them for over twenty, ten, and five years. All four families have seen the long-term picture—what happens as their children approach and enter adulthood.

While all of these families have different configurations, they are not all totally diverse—that could get too confusing. All four families are socioeconomically somewhere in the middle class. These families do not share the added struggles that come when parents do not have enough money . . . or when there is far more than enough. There are no stay-at-home mothers, although many moms in our society continue to give of themselves in that way. All the families have working parents, and have been touched by a parent's job changes during the last five years. All the families have children who are currently in their teens or older. All the families have at least one college-educated parent, and some have advanced degrees.

On the other hand, these families represent different ethnic groups. Three of the parents are bilingual. The numbers, ages, and relations of the children are different within the various families. The personality styles of the individuals are different. And, as with all our fellow humans, every family member has quirks and ways that make him or her unique.

John and Dot Singleton have been together for thirteen years. Both were once married to other people. They are the parents of a blended family: his family plus her family, including three girls and two boys. No children are actually his *and* hers. Their kids' ages range from the twenties into the thirties and they are in careers or are finishing school.

Kate and Carl bring two cultural perspectives to their marriage. Kate grew up in a family where interacting with the extended family was a daily affair; Carl was raised with his twin brother as an adopted child with very different definitions of togetherness. They have two children. Their daughter is in her mid-twenties, working on her own. Their son has just entered college.

Mapita is a single parent. Her marriage ended during its early years, and she has not remarried. She has raised two children, twin boys, on her own, receiving very little support from her former husband. Strongly influenced by her upbringing as a Latina, she has navigated through many situations that call for sensitive handling of cultural differences. Her boys are now in their first year of college.

Will and Margaret have been married for thirty years, but they didn't have children until they'd been married for ten years. Both of them grew up in the Midwest, in families that attended churches of the same denomination and had many of the same surface cultural values. They have learned that other things, such as gender or personality style, affect perspectives on raising children. Will comes from a family with only sons, Margaret is from a family of daughters. They have lived in their small western city for twenty-four years. Their daughter is now twenty-one years old, and their son is in high school.

The Tao not only serves as a framework for wise attitudes and behaviors but also helps to explain why some common practices are not particularly good. Over the years, after interacting with many moms and dads in a wide variety of settings, I have seen behaviors that are inappropriate, or even harmful, toward children. Some practices are simply unacceptable if we want students to learn and grow to be fulfilled adults.

I want parents who yell at their children, telling them such things as: "I wish I'd never had you," to change their attitudes. I am anxious to stop parents from offering love as a reward or punishment for social conduct: "If you get pregnant, you will never step foot in this house again." I want parents to stop using empty threats: "You won't leave your room for a month if you aren't home by twelve." I wish that parents could more easily see the effects of remarks as casual as: "Getting a little pudgy, aren't you?" I am anxious for parents to do their jobs well, so that children can learn to cope as adults with times of great change and disturbances. I am hopeful that parents will take to heart the importance of their own modeling. I will be grateful when parents acknowledge that their children may all be treated differently, in spite of their similarities, but that overt favoritism is never acceptable.

The best parenting may not look like parenting, because it resembles flying a kite. (Go fly a kite and see if the comparison is correct for you.)

Many people have asked me if Taoist belief is in conflict with other religions, such as Christianity. I usually respond by describing the dual avenues of Taoism. Over the centuries, Taoism as a *religion* has promoted some practices that would be inconsistent with the ways of other organized groups. Most religions do not advocate such things as fortune-telling, for example. On the other hand, the principles of ancient Taoism as a *philosophy* seem to be consistent with those of many other philosophies. In the *Tao Te Ching*, the roots of Taoism are clear, unblemished by any of the intervening centuries of religious disagreements, invented bodily practices, or mysticism.

The precepts I present in each of this book's eighty-one chapters are selected. In the *Tao Te Ching*, each chapter contains multiple concepts, and many are repeated from one chapter to the next. The idea of simplicity, for example, is stressed in at least twenty chapters. In order to emphasize messages and avoid being redundant, I have chosen certain ideas from each chapter and left others to be addressed in other chapters. Most of the opening maxims are identical to those originally written for *The Tao of Teaching*; I am convinced that good teaching and good parenting have much in common.

Someone who wants more information about how to implement the Tao at home might well go beyond this volume in order to find further ideas and practices. The list of books that follows this introduction names six books that I recommend highly. These can get you started—there are many more. Although these titles may seem rather Western in their popular orientation, you should find that they are appropriate if you are looking for extended understanding of and philosophical compatibility with the teachings of the Tao.

If you were to read other books by these authors, you would enjoy them too. I also think it is important that you not try too hard to understand the Tao immediately; it is better that your understanding come slowly and naturally. I have only included one book about the Tao, but you will be able to find many more (hundreds, for sure) when you wish.

What most of us come to learn is that we may *know* many good ideas related to parenting, but it is difficult to apply and *follow* our own advice, even if it is good. It is also frequently hard for couples to parent harmoniously when visions from their own early models in life are different. I hope that in reading the stories of this book, you will see that wise parenting is seldom perfect, is always tricky, and must be perceived with humor and hopefulness. Remember that sometimes the best parenting is "nonparenting." I hope that the stories about Dot and John, Carl and Kate, Mapita, and Will and Margaret will provide you with some clear models of ways in which you will be able to reveal your own good parenting beliefs.

- Dot and John Singleton: her daughter Natalie, her son Joe and his daughters Polly and Irma, his son Ralph
- Carl and Kate Flanagan: daughter Holly, son Corey
- Mapita Sanchez: sons Jacob and Samuel
- Lew and Margaret Williams: daughter Cynthia, son Patrick

No single book can meet any parent's needs. The stories in this book are mainly about events that affect parents in the middle class. You may have concerns that take you beyond this book and these middle-class families. Your family will benefit from consulting a wide range of resources. Other books abound. I have provided a short list for you myself. Parenting newsletters and parenting newspapers are common. Perhaps your doctor's office carries free copies. There are many other parents around you to talk with. Schools, medical centers, and religious institutions offer parenting courses. You can also learn a great deal by listening to others and watching carefully. And you can learn through reflection on what *you* have done well and what you'd like to do better. Take the time to think about your good fortune in being a parent. And I hope that you will decide to read this book.

Do not hesitate to write to me if you have ideas to share or questions to pose. I wish you well in your journey. In closing, I have two wishes for you. Enjoy your children. Relax.

—Greta K. Nagel

Recommended Reading

Ginott, Haim G. (1969). *Between Parent and Teenager.* New York: Avon Books. This classic has wonderful vignettes that can help you to think of positive, nonaggressive ways to speak in a great variety of situations.

Goldberg, Natalie (1986). *Writing Down the Bones.* Boston: Shambhala. You may be surprised at this one. It isn't about parenting; it is a very readable book about writing for you to enjoy. Yes, you. It is good not to pay constant close attention to your parenting, and it is wise to reflect and explore your own creativity. Grow in attentiveness to detail. Have a good read, and jot down a few things about your family.

Keirsey, Ken, and Marilyn Bates (1984). *Please Understand Me.* Del Mar, CA: Gnosology. Human interactions are affected by the personality styles of the individuals involved. Learn about your own preferences and tendencies as you attempt to understand others'.

McGinnis, Alan Loy (1985). *Bringing Out the Best in People.* Minneapolis: Augsburg. Leading a family is not exactly like leading a corporation. At many times it is more difficult. This book will help you to take some time out to think.

Nagel, Greta K. (1994). *The Tao of Teaching.* New York: Donald I. Fine and Primus. This volume illustrates the Tao as three teachers incorporate it in their practices.

Peck, M. Scott (1978). *The Road Less Traveled.* New York: Simon and Schuster. Expanding the capacity to love extends the capacity to grow.

1. The way is nameless; the name is not the way

A wise parent does not parent by anyone else's book. Mothers and fathers give up much when they attach a particular label, such as Dr. Spock, developmental, or tough love, to their styles of raising children. Instead, in the Tao, parents make choices and use ideas that are warranted because of the needs, values, interests, and personalities of their children and of themselves as parents. In the Tao it is important to maintain individuality. Names are limiting, for other people's definitions are attached to those names.

Listening to the advice of friends, grandparents, and other relatives can also be nervewracking for parents at any stage. When the baby is new, each person will recommend the best book or program for everything from the birth itself to diaper-changing to feeding to sleeping. When preschool and school enrollment decisions are made, there are dozens of education books to explore in regular bookstores and more to be found in teacher supply stores. When the children start acting like children and the teens start acting like teens, parents are frequently referred to an assortment of services, articles, or volumes.

Clarify the ideals of your own carefully developed philosophy. There you will discover the seeds for the many decisions that must be made in a family.

Even though Lew and Margaret have differences of opinion about specific child raising techniques, they have always agreed on the values that they cherish for their children. Lew never bought the idea of formal timeouts, but he and Margaret always agreed that it was best to have children cool off before discussing problems. Margaret thinks that children should have time limits on their TV schedule, but she agrees with her husband that the kids need to learn to organize their own time and lives. Lew believes in guidelines, but not rules. Margaret thinks that rules, as long as they are created together, are fine. Both parents believe that children should live with encouragement, not criticism, and they struggle to make that a reality.

In their family, the children assume responsibility in many ways. Cynthia and Patrick, their daughter and son, have made their own choices about various issues at all stages of life. It isn't always easy for the kids, but they know that they may always seek help from their parents.

During their early years, as each of their birthdays approached, Cynthia or Patrick would choose a theme for the party, decide who would come to the celebration, and draw the invitations that were sent to the guests. Margaret and Lew have stepped in when there was an oversight, such as a good friend left off the guest list, but their comments are mostly inquisitive. (Is there a reason James isn't on the list? Are you sure you want to wear one black sock and one blue? Aren't pajamas better for *in* the house?) No comment questions a child's character or intelligence.

Margaret and Lew know that they haven't been alone in raising their children. They realized along the way that their children's relatives, teachers, babysitters, parents of friends, group leaders, coaches, and religious leaders have all been influential. They are grateful for how many good people their kids have gotten to know as they've grown. As Cynthia and Patrick mature, the values that have "stuck" have become clear. They have confidence in themselves, and they know that it is OK to be different and not always go with the crowd. They both respect differences in others and are open to new experiences.

Living with those ideals isn't always easy for Lew and Margaret.

They've been uncomfortable when their children show up in unusual hairdos, when they wear strange combinations of worn, thrift shop clothes, or when they decide not to join the mainstream activities that Mom or Dad joined in their youth. But the children have accepted the important values that Lew and Margaret wanted to pass on to them. Cynthia and Patrick have very distinctive styles and interests, but they both demonstrate initiative and stick-to-it-iveness. They follow through on commitments to others, and when they work on special projects or paying jobs, things get done, and done well.

Both kids have learned to read, speak, and write well. Teachers offer compliments each year: "Cynthia has been a wonderful science student," or "I've never had a student who could write poetry as well as Patrick." The children enjoy reading books, and they both like to spend their allowance money on books for themselves and for others. They are both very creative; they've made paintings and drawings that decorate the walls at home, and both Lew and Margaret have the children's work hanging by their desks at work.

Both kids have also gotten involved in community activities, including feeding the homeless in their town. Cynthia has spent long hours helping at the local hospital in the emergency room and with brain-injured patients, as well as helping with menial chores at a nursing home in a nearby city.

Do not follow the dictates of any one method. One may know the insights of the Way without having to give it a name.

2. Silence is a virtue

Parents who talk too much to (or at) their children often cause them to tune out or to rebel by arguing or being disobedient. Once family agreements have been made to do things a certain way, based on shared values, a wise parent should expect certain results. In the Tao, parents do not constantly remind their children of things, nor do they harp on past mistakes. When agreements are not kept, natural consequences are part of the Way. Reflections about the quality of children's accomplishments are best shared through brief, specific compliments and encouragements for children to do self-reflection.

Although it is hard to be quiet, do not admonish harshly nor lecture repeatedly. Speak once, and expect to be heard.

Divorced early in her marriage, Mapita has raised her twin sons by herself since they were six months old. Her experiences as a public school teacher who has worked with hundreds of students in her career serve her daily as a parent. She knows that she must avoid too much talking, for if the children feel nagged, the impact of the message is lost. When working with students, she knows that in order to help bring about change, she must choose a focus issue and address it. It does no good to talk about many problems at once.

At home, Mapita knows that the best times to speak are either when a situation is fresh—or at least fresh in everyone's mind—or when the boys are asking for her to comment. Her silence is always a sign of reflection, and sometimes it is a signal that she is angry as well. Silent times allow her to really think about things from more than one perspective.

When the boys were teenagers, they were very involved in activities at their high school. One Saturday, after Mapita wouldn't let Jacob go out with his friends because he had been gone many evenings in a row, he erupted and yelled at her. "You never listen to me! You never let me do anything!" When his outburst ended, she turned and walked into the garage in silence and busied herself sorting and washing clothes.

It took Jacob several hours, but he came over to her that evening, wanting to talk. At first, he acknowledged that he had yelled at her, but he did not apologize.

Mapita's calm response was: "In our house, I won't yell at

you, but at the same time you must not yell at me because I am your mother. This is the way our family has done things. I didn't yell at my mother and my mother didn't yell at me. This is our home. This should be our safe place." And that was that.

Several months later, Jacob was at home, missing a day at school, and missing a trip with his wrestling team, because he was sick with bronchitis. His friend Willy came in the house and started to yell at him. "What do you think you're doing?! You're letting the team down! You can't stay home!" Jacob's response was concise: "Stop yelling. No one yells in this house. I chose to stay home to get well and it is my decision."

Good parenting can mean few words.

3. Wealth breeds competition

Where wealth holds power, one often finds contests. Our children live in a society where winning is everything. Bumper stickers on our cars announce that the family's child is the citizen of the month at the local school. Some address materialism with humor. "The one who dies with the most toys wins." One bumper even shows off a sign saying, "I want to be Barbie. That bitch has everything." Television commercials and magazines promote being the first on the block to own things. Such competition is compelling for children because it is compelling for adults.

In some areas, parents encourage competitiveness in sports. Other neighborhoods seem to drill in the need to be the top student, attending the top colleges. In other areas, where more money is prominent, families compete to have the most material goods—the most expensive clothes, the biggest house, the latest electronic gadgets.

In the spring of their child's prekindergarten year, some parents push for acceptance in private schools, celebrating admis-

sion to the "right" school with champagne or challenging a school's decision if a child happens not to make the list. In elementary school, the contests are often part of the explicit school culture. Children win bicycles and CD players for selling goods that help fund their school programs; they win pizza for reading books. On through the grades, the phenomenon remains, only the nature of the contests change. At the same time, other contests are implicit; whoever wears the clothes or shoes with the best labels or has the most CDs or the fanciest video system is a "winner."

In the Tao, children are compared with themselves, not with friends and classmates. They can be saved the anguish and conflict of constant competition with others. Parents invite their children to enter into the process of deciding what things they like to do that don't require buying expensive items. They buy things that will support activity and creativity, follow up on interests, and promote positive social interactions.

Honor other values over wealth and trendy acquisitions to help free your children from competition and to help free you to pursue a calm life. Say yes with caution, say no with care.

When Corey was a young boy, his parents noticed that plastic hero figures and matchbox cars always played important roles in his imaginary play. His productions would last for hours in the gray dirt landscapes that he created in the back yard. He would create half a dozen car sound effects with buzzing, vibrating lips as he spoke the parts of dozens of characters, good and bad. "Heh-heh-heh, I've got you now! I'll get YOU! Take THAT!" While other children were content to watch TV, Corey spent his free time outside in physical and imaginary play. Carl and Kate allowed him to purchase plastic figures and small cars rather regularly, and his toys allowed for creativity and entertainment at an exceptionally good price.

As Corey grew older, he began to ask for the kinds of video games and hand-held video sets that were becoming popular at the time. His parents decided that, even though they had enough money to purchase those items, plenty of things were just as enjoyable, not as costly, and more long-lasting. When Corey was in sixth grade he and his friend John enjoyed ordering from a mail-order catalog of gags—fake hands and packs of gum, ice cubes that contained houseflies, whoopee cushions. His favorite was the trick camera. As he told a family friend at the time, "It looks just like the cameras that shoot water when you press the button, and *everyone* is on to that trick. So when you take out the camera, sure enough, your friend will say, 'Oh, Corey, let me take *your* picture.' And with this new camera, you act dumb and say, 'Sure, here.' Then they hold the camera up to their eye to take your picture, and when they push the button it squirts on *them* instead. Ha, ha, ha, ha."

The items that Carl and Kate bought for Corey as presents were also relatively simple kinds of things. He liked it when gifts at holidays and birthdays were really surprises, so he never complained when the actual present wasn't the exact one he'd requested. Carl and Kate made sure that if they did not give Corey the specifically-asked-for gift, the substitute had to be thoughtful. They were items that met his special interests and were chosen with care to provide opportunities for activity and creativity. As it happened, Corey played with friends who had video games at home, and they liked to visit his house because of the different things they could do there. And along the way, everyone in the family noticed how quickly certain electronic games and systems went out of style.

When Holly was in junior high, brand name fashions were the thing: everyone simply had to have Sergio Valenti jeans, Farrah Fawcett hair, Esprit shoes, and clothes by Calvin Klein and Guess. Holly was expected to stay within the family budget for clothes, so she kept her pricey acquisitions to a minimum. On a couple of occasions, she visited her Aunt Tina in San Francisco and was allowed to buy a few high-priced items at a brand-name outlet. When it was time to select her graduation dress, her parents reminded her that although eighth-grade graduation marked a transition, it was not considered a major milestone in their family. Many of Holly's friends were going to be dressed for graduation in strapless taffeta dresses. Their gowns were beautiful shades of yellow, lime, blue, and white; extravagant and expensive. Holly's parents encouraged her to find a conservative dress, that was simple enough to wear somewhere else.

Kate took Holly to a number of stores to look at a variety of dresses. The dress that Holly chose was made of peach crepe and was simple, modest, and straight, with short sleeves and a plain scoop neckline. She could just relax, be herself . . . and not worry about a revealing dress that might fall down. It wasn't costly and it wasn't fancy. Nevertheless, everyone loved it. Other kids, teachers, friends' parents, and complete strangers walked up to Holly that night and complimented her. She was "elegant"; she'd kept it simple.

Relaxation requires no competition.

4. Function and substance are both important

In the Tao, parents involve their children in activities that are part of daily life. Parents can seldom "pour in" knowledge. It is acquired more readily when it flows from experiences. Children love to learn and are adept at retaining information when they understand how it relates to their lives.

The lessons that wise parents teach seldom seem like "parenting" because they are intimately involved with how the family survives and grows. Supermarket shopping trips are necessary parts of life for most families. Parents who insist that their children stay at home because "they might beg for treats" miss seeing the big picture. As long as trips are scheduled when nobody is starving, appropriate behaviors are discussed ahead of time, and the trip doesn't have to be rushed, these trips can be excellent learning experiences. Young children will come to know about foods and workers in the community; teenagers can learn about the value of money and about nutritional aspects of various foods.

Involve your children in activities that can enrich their lives intellectually and personally for the present and the future. Always be able to answer for yourself and demonstrate for the children: "Why are we doing this?" When the Tao is applied, its depths have no end.

When the twins were in elementary school, they always went to the supermarket to do the grocery shopping with Mapita. She remembers that they were so busy with little adventures, they usually forgot to beg for sweets. "Find the flour in aisle 8 for us, please. See if you can find the salsa. Can you find Jonathan apples? Which box of spaghetti has the least calories? Please choose about five dollars' worth of soup for us. We need more Mexican chocolate for hot chocolate. We have coupons for two cereals. Can you find them?" At first, the boys seemed to be on a treasure hunt. Later, as they grew, they were each given a part of the family shopping list to gather. Mapita taught them how to use aisle numbers correctly, identifying categories and subcategories of groceries. She also taught them tricks about choosing ripe avocados and planning low-calorie meals, and she showed them how to seek out seasonal fruits and the most reasonable, nutritious rice. Keeping the kitchen cabinets and refrigerator well stocked on a single parent's income was a family endeavor; finding the most healthy food for the money was a family enterprise.

Supermarket shopping became second nature to Samuel and Jacob. As teenagers, they took over much of the weekly shopping. Their regimen for wrestling meant that they had to eat very carefully in order to stay at proper weights. They got to know two supermarkets well. One was great for produce. The other had better prices for canned and packaged goods like cereal.

In addition, the household finances in general became part of the boys' business when they entered their teens. They were as familiar with the bills that came to their mailbox as Mapita. Not only did she believe in "no secrets," but she found that it was simply good sense for the boys to open the bills and examine the costs of everything from electricity to the telephone. How things went in one area always affected what could be spent in another, and soon the reasons for economizing became crystal clear.

Jacob always checked the family budget in order to decide whether to take a girl out for a restaurant dinner or a picnic. Picnics became common in his social calendar, because a meal at his favorite Italian restaurant could run five times more. He really enjoyed preparing a picnic, complete with the foods that he knew his date would love, such as a seasoned rice dish along with chicken, and strawberry smoothies, as well as dishes that he knew that he would enjoy, such as pizza and Italian cannoli. The whole combination meal could be topped off with oranges and ice cream.

Application breeds learning; dig deeply.

5. Be impartial

All people are "straw dogs" in the Tao, no person more important than others. Many parents practice favoritism, showing greater enjoyment in some children than in others, extending favors to some but not others. Quite often the children who remind the parents of themselves (whether accurately or not) because of a match in personality, style, interests, or values are the ones who receive extra attention and manage to gain extra favors. But when children are troublesome, parents aggravate problems when they compare or threaten. We hear comments like: "Why can't you be like your sister?" or "Your brother never put us through that." We hear about wayward children being disowned and difficult offspring being disinherited.

Wise parents are aware of the many effects of differences in areas such as gender personality. They reach out to find points of empathy with all their children and know that treating children with equal attention doesn't always mean identical attention. One child may require lots of driving; another craves time at home; yet another may want your support, but at a distance.

Encourage all your children with your time, efforts, and sense of shared responsibility. Look for ways to stress equality. Never trade in words that belittle your wife or husband or your sons or daughters. In a family, there are no winners if one member loses.

Margaret and Lew both grew up in families where opportunities and advantages were provided to all the children in equal doses. Margaret and her two sisters were given the opportunity to go to college; Lew and his two brothers were all sent to college as well. That had not always been the case in earlier generations of their families; some of the children had been allowed to go to college, and some weren't. It had always seemed unfair that Lew's mom had to go to work at an office job in order to help her two brothers get through school, even though she was an interested and capable student. Margaret had always wondered why few of her nine aunts and uncles went to college.

Cynthia and Patrick understand their parents' desire to give them equal treatment in matters large, such as school, or small, such as holiday presents or special treats. It goes without saying that Lew and Margaret will support both their children through the college (or the equivalent) educations of their choice.

In lesser arenas, the kids are good at teasing their parents whenever something doesn't appear quite equivalent. "He got more presents than I did," Cynthia moaned, with a smile on her face, after her brother's graduation from junior high. Margaret replied, "Do you recall that your school never *had* a graduation? It went through ninth grade at that time? Hmmmm? You didn't have announcements and you didn't have a ceremony. Right?" Several months later when Patrick was a freshman in high school: "You never let *me* watch R-rated movies when I was his age," Cynthia complained. Margaret reminded her that Patrick wasn't allowed to either. The policy hadn't changed, even if a slip-up had occurred. Patrick grumbled, "You sent Cynthia to Space Camp." Lew asked him, "Do *you* want to go?" Patrick's response: "No."

Lew and Margaret know that since there is one girl in the family, it's okay to say, "You're our favorite daughter." Since there is only one boy, they may say, "Our favorite son." And they do.

Do not play favorites. All are creatures, some great and some small.

6. The Way will never wear out with use

Just as the mind does not wear out from being used, the Way never becomes old or boring. Its growth is based upon frequent use as well as new, creative ideas.

Over and over again, the choices that parents and children make together in respect for one another do not get old. They get better. Children and parents deepen their relationships through activities that occur over and over as well as through enjoying one another's inventiveness. The Tao is not inextricably bound to strict schedules nor to anyone's idea as to what must be done at every moment. At times, everyone may be doing the same thing, but in a different way for they are individuals. At other times, everyone may be the same in that they are doing different things.

You will see that being in the Tao means never being exhausted.

When John and Dot married, they wanted their children from their respective previous marriages to have good times together, casual experiences in which relationships could develop naturally. The family frequently made short trips to the desert. During the years before this second marriage, John had started to create a "place," five acres with a small wooden house out in the middle of the Mojave Desert. Nothing fancy, it was the sort of retreat where friends could visit and, if they wanted to, could expect to spend time pounding nails, adding something here or there on to a building that grew in bits and pieces. The main activities there were exploring the surrounding desert, eating very simple meals, and sitting in front of a campfire at night. The desert visits were an important part of the growing process for their new family. To Dot's way of thinking, "If it builds our family and provides a sense of community, it is something to be done."

The five children, ages seven through sixteen at the time, thought these times in the desert were wonderful. They explored the surrounding landscape inch by inch, learning that all those brown lizards and green cacti had special names and identities. Over time, the kids learned a few scientific names and even handed out a few proper names of their own to the local residents. The lizard who always seemed to sit by the kitchen door became Pal.

When the kids went off on long walks, they would come back with bunches of sage that they would tightly bundle with string to throw on the campfire at night. Colorful gourds grew nearby, and the children brought the most beautiful ones back to decorate the cabin in orange, yellow, and green. The older children were allowed to go off on their bikes, distancing themselves from their parents in adventures that took them into safe but untracked territory for hours.

Many afternoons, just sitting around was fine. All the family members enjoyed reading, and all the kids were into arts and crafts of one sort or another. Polly loved to draw pictures of people and horses, and Irma could spend hours arranging small rocks in categories and patterns. She also loved to put the interior of the cabin in order—straightening furniture, dusting, even arranging the various collected gourds in still-life groupings around the open kitchen-living room. Natalie loved to sit and read in the old converted water tower cover turned upside down to hold a pool warmed by the sun. Joe and Ralph could spend hours together, examining wind-blown bits of wood or metal artifacts from old cabins. They also learned to build roofs and windows under John's watchful eye.

Each night, when millions of stars were bright and white against the black night sky, the boys built a bonfire in a ring near the side of the house. John always started singing good old songs by the fire. Everyone sang, and songs like "This Land Is Your Land," "Leavin' on a Jet Plane," or "I've Been Workin' on the Railroad" floated from their throats into the vast night.

After a dozen songs or more, everyone would tell stories they'd heard at camp or repeat jokes they'd heard at school. Ghost stories were okay, and even "knock knock" jokes could be delivered without a moan or a groan because of the way everyone was accepting of one another out there.

Back in the cabin, a board game might be pulled out. Old sets of *Monopoly* and *Scrabble* were always available, and eventually the skills and talents of one person or the other would emerge. One time they played a game called *Scruples*. It provided a time to talk about moral stances as well as enjoy playing a game together. Comments never fell on deaf ears.

"I can't believe you would really do that!"

"Would you, really?"

"I think I'd probably do the same thing."

One night, when other families were guests at the desert place, about twenty people, young and old, blew out the candles in the cabin and played *Murder at Midnight*.

For both the children and the grownups, these getaway times offered chances to experience the simple joys of nature and wildlife in the desert and get to know each other better and better.

In the Tao, allow things to unfold.

7. Do not think of self

In the Tao, parents think of their children first.

What interests you, the parent, is not unimportant, but it cannot come first all the time. When you show your children that you care about them, they will return your interest. Providing regular, undivided attention to each child is a hallmark of wise parenting. Certainly, responsible parents meet their obligations to their jobs. They also set aside some time for pastimes that bring personal enrichment and rejuvenation. In addition, they attend to critical household chores. Time for the children, however, comes ahead, not instead of, the other important things to do. Sometimes parents find enjoyable ways to include their children as they attend to other responsibilities. Make individual "dates" with your children to do things that are uniquely pleasing to them. You will be fulfilled.

Raising twin boys presented many challenges to Mapita. As a single parent, she recognized that she had to play the roles and do the work of two people. At first, she did not trust her ability to handle two active youngsters. When Samuel and Jacob were toddlers, she kept the living room clear of most furniture. The coffee table she had owned for several years prior to her brief marriage had sharp corners and curved iron legs that protruded dangerously from beneath a glass surface. She sold it. Plates and statues from her visits to foreign countries were made of fragile painted pottery and precious porcelain. She wrapped them up and put them away into closets and cabinets for over seven years. The only furniture that was allowed to remain in the living room was a soft, blue, well-worn sofa.

The Sanchez boys knew that they could depend on their mom to be there for them. There was never any doubt in *her* mind that the boys would be successful students in public school. She was very involved in her sons' education, visiting the teachers and principal if necessary. And although she has always been a strong supporter of teachers, she made sure that she listened with care and asked questions at conferences to make sure that her children were being treated fairly. She has never doubted that her time spent at school has been extremely valuable.

Mapita worked hard, sometimes at two jobs at once, in order to provide her kids with clothes, sports equipment, and school supplies. When she was at work, she wanted the very best child care for her boys. She decided early on that it would work best for her to have someone come to their home, so she hired a woman who would care for the kids in their own environment. Mapita also knew that she wanted her children to maintain their abilities with her family's traditional primary language, so she hired someone who would speak Spanish with the boys during the day.

When Mapita's own work day was over, her family came before other social obligations. She had many friendships, including many she made through her work, but she wouldn't allow her social life to take her time and energy away from her family. Life consisted of simple dinners, enjoying relatives, having friends over, and going places where the boys could go too.

When Jacob and Samuel were in their junior year of high school, Mapita realized that her job was interfering with her family life. She didn't like the fact that teaching adults and putting on workshops at night and on weekends meant that she was gone from home at the very times when the boys were home. She knew that college was ahead for both of them, and that they would probably be leaving home for college at the end of their senior year. So, with her priorities clear, she decided to go back to daytime public school teaching, work that she had done well at the beginning of her career.

Being there for the twins wasn't always convenient. Sometimes they assumed that they had their mother's time without checking with her calendar. Mapita made plans to meet a school friend for lunch one Super Bowl Sunday, not knowing that the boys had already made elaborate plans that included her. They had invited ten people over for a Super Bowl party, with plenty of Mexican food, including homemade mole and tamales from a nearby restaurant, in addition to plenty of chips and junk food. The boys had also invited two adult family friends so that Mapita would have plenty of company during the afternoon. Mapita gave up her lunch date, but she had a fine time.

From the time they were six months old, Samuel and Jacob were given quality time *and* quantity time at home. Mapita has never begrudged the time she has devoted to meeting their needs. It does not always make for perfectly smooth sailing in her other relationships, but her choices have allowed her to focus on her real priority.

Put yourself behind; you will end up ahead.

8. Do not promote competition, and be careful with words

Sibling rivalry has been around for a long, long time. In telling one child that she or he is a "great kid," a parent leaves the other to think that he or she isn't great. The child who earns no compliment is no winner.

Reprimands can also carry a variety of messages to children. Teaching a lesson to one in the view of the other doesn't always teach the same lesson to the second child. If a parent compares one child to the other ("Your sister would never do that! Why can't you be more like your brother?"), it can cause resentment and denial. If a parent points out one child's flaws many times a day and never chastises the other child for anything, the criticized child will feel he's being treated unfairly. Even tone of voice can be a problem. Parents sometimes use "sweet talk" with a favored child and harsh commands and questions with another. Some may say that one child "deserves" the criticism. No child de-

serves criticism; *all children deserve encouragement and a sense of the right things to do in various situations. In addition, children need guidance and correction.*

Compliments are important. Make them specific, and don't use them as bribes. ("I sure do appreciate the hard work you put into cleaning your room." "The hours you spent on the painting paid off. It looks professional.") Do not always make them in the presence of other children. Save reprimands for private times. Keep corrections simple and identify the positive behaviors that will be better choices. ("When you don't do your homework, you are saying that it isn't important. We can all talk to your teacher if you need more challenging assignments.") Make promises you can keep, and keep those promises. All are tokens of your unconditional love.

When Holly was in elementary school, Kate and Carl noticed that when their daughter came home from school, she liked to go into her room and start sketching. She could spend hours at her desk with her drawing pad, and getting her to stop was sometimes a chore. She also loved to play with Legos. Instead of watching TV, she was happy to design and build all sorts of structures during her elementary school years. Carl and Kate not only complimented her but often discovered themselves down on the floor creating things with her.

The Flanagans also noticed that Holly actually enjoyed doing her homework. Every assignment was a special event, and she became well known at the local stationery store, for she was a frequent buyer of art supplies, plastic report covers and page sleeves, and stickers. Various homework assignments, not just reports, went back to school looking attractive and interesting, with added artwork, interesting cover pages, and "professional" display notebooks.

Corey, on the other hand, was not interested in the same things as Holly. School was all right. Homework was something to be done. Drawing with Dad was fun . . . sometimes. Carl and Kate knew that they had to be careful not to hold Holly up as an example, as a big sister who had to be emulated. Her artistic ways and her techniques for school success were unique to her. Corey's strengths were very different, and some were not always obvious to his parents. Corey was a social person who liked being entertained. He liked scary books. Recess was great because he loved to run around. In school it was hard for him to sit still and pay attention for long stretches of time.

Corey told a family friend when he was a sixth-grader, "The most important thing about school is your teacher. It is pretty bad if your teacher is boring." He was worried about his teacher who "talks too slowly, so you fall asleep by the time she says, 'Boys . . . and . . . girls . . . take . . . your . . . books . . . out.' " By the time he got into seventh grade, he was bored with the ways of his school. As Carl and Kate put it, he started to "goof off." His grades went down, and although he was never disrespectful, he was frequently inattentive. Conferences with his teacher were not disastrous, for he was a good kid, after all. Still, both his parents and teacher were concerned.

Kate and Carl saw that things were not easy for Corey during eighth grade at all. Nevertheless, they resisted the temptation to point at Holly's ongoing school successes. She was on the road to becoming her school's valedictorian at the time, but it was foolish to indulge in any "Why can't you be like your sister" talk.

When it came time to pick a high school, Corey wanted to go where he was not going to have to attend classes with all his classmates from grade school. He wanted to get away from some of the kids he had known for a long, long time and to make new friends. He wanted to go to a parochial high school that two of his older cousins attended. His parents agreed that he could follow in their footsteps.

When he got to ninth grade at his new high school, Corey went out for football for the first time in his life. In spite of the fact that he was a complete novice, his family was supportive, his coach was encouraging, and his teammates were patient. His team was the "white team"—the team for inexperienced players. It was not easy for Corey. Over and over, he had to work hard and suffer through injuries, aches and pains. Nevertheless, as Carl and Kate observed, he really enjoyed football and was good at it. His newfound confidence and persistence began to spill over into many aspects of his life. A front-page newspaper article written about Corey his senior year named him as the county lineman of the year. Then he went on to be named the outstanding lineman of the year for Southern California. Both Corey and his parents were pleasantly surprised at how his hard work paid off.

Kate and Carl believed that when children received awards, the best thing for them to do was to recognize the honor and compliment the hard work and dedication that went into achieving the award. By honoring that behavior, it became clear that any other family member could also be an award recipient. Just having a talent wasn't the important thing—making an effort was.

Words may not break bones, but they can break hearts.

9. The material is fleeting, the spiritual is everlasting

The Tao recognizes that good parenting is not dependent on fancy things or materialistic values. Parents can provide experiences for their children that show them a way to honor, share with, and give to other people. Human powers go beyond mere physical force. Developing children's recognition of values and beliefs in life is a slow, but rewarding process.

Help your children see the aspects of life that go beyond the surface of daily living and celebrations—beyond toys, furniture, and clothing. Permit them to find out about your understandings of the deeper dimensions of life. Begin by drawing out the goodness toward others that already exists within your sons and daughters.

When Dot and John brought their two families together, their feelings were strong and they cared deeply about one another. They recognized, though, that their new marriage was not just a matter of their devotion to one another. It would be successful if their two families could learn to care about one another and about the world around them. To help bring them closer together, Dot declared "family night" one night each week.

Family night wasn't on any specific day of the week for the Singletons. Instead, everyone looked at their schedules of lessons and sports and school activities and made a decision for that coming week or month. Each family member had an opportunity to suggest the evening's activities, so some of the evenings were away from home. If something special was going on at the school, the whole family would scramble into the family station wagon and go to see it together. Sometimes a family night was like a field trip and included going to a professional play at the county repertory theater or traveling to the planetarium in the next city. The night might even be a walk on the beach or a trip to the mall for school clothes.

Nevertheless, the family nights spent at home were the most common variety and were probably the most memorable nights for everyone. A big part of the special time was having everyone together to share a good dinner.

Friends would ask John and Dot what they did about the kids' homework on family nights, knowing fully that the Singletons value education highly. They were surprised by the response. Homework was important but not as high a priority as family. If a homework project couldn't be completed within the hours outside the time devoted to family night, Dot or John would write a note to the proper teacher, and the homework always managed to get done for the next day.

During the early years of their newly formed family, John and Dot also served as the advisors for the youth group at their church. The whole family went along to most meetings and outings, even the children who weren't quite youth-group age. Many activities kept them all busy at the church, sharing dinners, performing in mini-plays for the congregation, collecting items for local food drives, and singing for the senior citizens homes in the area. Some church projects took them long distances; one important one was the annual backpacking trip. Everyone piled into cars and trucks and headed up the eastern side of the Sierra Mountains. Each group or family had their own camping gear, and each person also had to carry the ingredients for one or two of the communal meals that they cooked at nine thousand feet.

Because of their involvement with the church, the Singleton family also coordinated more than ten trips to help an orphanage in Baja, Mexico. The whole family would drive down together, carrying food, diapers, and clothing, as well as tools and materials for fixing things. When they arrived at the orphanage they would find a space in the yard and set up a big tent that held sleeping bags for all seven family members. Then they set about holding babies, painting buildings, pulling weeds, planting flowers, and fixing things for the ninety or so children at that particular orphanage. Everyone played baseball with the kids, and because there might be as many as twenty other visitors staying there, games were pretty noisy and exciting. Dot's Spanish came in handy, but the fact that not everyone knew the language of the Mexican children did not dampen their spirits or keep them all from interacting.

Honor and integrity are not "out there"; they come from within. Learn to be free of unnecessary constraints in order to connect with others.

10. Do not be authoritarian

Wise parents have authority but do not choose to be authoritarian. They are respected by their children as part of a family whose members work for the betterment of the whole group.

They do not insist that children rely on them to make their decisions or to tell them how to do their work. Parents in the Tao do not demand that the children follow their dictates blindly. However, once an agreement is made, there are reasonable consequences for not following through.

The father who always yells things like: "This is the fourth time I've reminded you to do the dishes! Get in here!" does his child no favor. Chores, and the memory to do them, are the responsibility of the child. Setting up deadlines with agreed-on consequences together may be a way to create a plan.

Find ways for your children to have power over what and how they achieve and to examine and reflect on what they have done. Do not expect or allow your children to rely on you for things that they can do well for themselves.

Margaret and Lew thought it was important for their children to learn to handle money. Cynthia earned money by baby-sitting, but she needed an additional source of income to meet her needs. Lew and Margaret had read a magazine article that talked about using allowances as tools to teach children about money management, so they devised a new allowance system for their daughter. They sat down with Cynthia and listed all the typical obligations that she had. She received her allowance once a month, enough to cover clothing, movies, birthday party gifts, and one CD a month. The only exceptions were for a school clothing bonus of $100 at the end of each summer, and then, as the years with the system rolled by, formal dresses for dances were also covered by parents.

Although Cynthia made some mistakes along the way, she found that having to manage the dollars and cents was fun. She experimented with different stores and different expenditures. She loved being able to buy more CDs in some months because she decided to and being able to buy a special outfit at another time because she had saved enough.

Cynthia went away to college feeling good about managing money and excited about her new checking account. She decided to avoid a credit card for her freshman year, but she later got one to establish a credit record, paying her total charges each month. She was thrifty about most things, sometimes almost "too thrifty" in her parents' minds, because she found thrift shop clothing so attractive.

Patrick also received his allowance as a money management opportunity. When he lost his orthodontic retainer, Margaret had him pay for half of it. After that, he was more careful about where he put it. He learned that financial mistakes hurt and that you must be careful with how you spend money and with the things you spend money on. In high school, he even began a personal campaign against overpriced brand-name clothing.

Do not expect others to rely on you.

11. Emptiness has usefulness

In the Tao, the concept of wu-wei *is that nonbeing has utility. The space in a bowl or cup, the opening in the hub of a wheel, and the vacant places of windows or doors in a building all serve important functions. Ideas of vacancy can help parents in several ways. The parent who asks a question and then does nothing actually does something very useful in providing time for children to think. A wise parent also engages in "reading between the lines," using intuition to determine what a child really means, even though the words or actions are not there. In addition, he or she knows that pauses in speaking or breaks in action can lend importance and meaning to words and actions.*

Most important, thoughtful parents know that children need "space." Mistaken are the parents who are ever-present, telling how and when tasks should be done or what to do in the future. Their children will not be able to make appropriate decisions on their own as they mature if they always turn to their parents.

Give your children the emptiness they need. Keep your interactions free of constant directives and keep options open for each individual. Be near, but far.

Mapita knows that, even though they're identical twins, each of her boys is a very complex individual with his own strengths, preferences, and idiosyncrasies. She has noticed traits develop over the years, but she has been very careful to encourage, rather than force, choices of activities on her sons. She knows that practicing emptiness doesn't mean doing nothing, but she is able to relax as the boys explore options.

When the boys were still preschoolers, she took them to a piano school that specialized in teaching young children to play the piano. The program included parent participation, and Mapita decided that she was willing to do what was necessary, not because the boys were going to be concert pianists, but so they could have a chance to see what they were really attracted to. Mapita figured that helping each of her sons to find his focus was an important investment of her time and money. She tried to find programs that offered things that she could afford. The schools offered instruction in musical instruments. The city offered programs in arts and crafts. Keeping the boys busy was always secondary in her mind to helping them to find their respective talents and interests.

As the boys grew, Mapita enjoyed watching and listening to their preferences and dreams.

Jacob has always been interested in social sorts of things. He really enjoys dealing with people of all ages and types. His dream is to get a house somewhere on the coast, maybe south of Newport Beach, California, where he would swim and sit on the beach and lounge around in lawn chairs with friends all day. He also could wrestle every day of his life. He is into science and mathematics, and he thinks that some day he just might go into business or international law. He loves to argue. He is also a great lover of music and films.

Samuel, on the other hand, is a lover of English, social studies, and the arts. He enjoys seeing films, like *Romeo and Juliet*, at least three times. He would love to sit and sip tea in the garden on a breezy summer day and then go out to dinner at an Italian restaurant with his family. He enjoys being a peacemaker.

As the boys ended their high school careers, Mapita knew that the future was theirs to decide. Each boy had several choices as to which college to attend and, once there, the road to selecting a major would be wide open.

So far, the journey for each boy has not been particularly predictable in foresight, just understandable in hindsight, and Mapita believes that that has been the best way.

Vacancy is an advantage.

12. Control input to the senses; avoid confusion and respond to inner depth

We soon learn in life that there can be too much of a good thing. Loud music is deafening. Excesses in food and drink can cause health problems. Working in direct sun can be too glaring; it limits our ability to concentrate. A wise parent provides a moderate environment that helps everyone to enjoy communication. A stimulating environment and lifestyle works for some personalities, but rushing through life, living with every day jam-packed with activity, precludes reflection.

Think about the ways in which your environment fosters positive family relations. Take time out just to relax with your family. Remember that individuals do need privacy at times. Times of repose allow times of action to be more meaningful.

During their high school years, Mapita's boys were popular at their school. They held leadership positions in sports and a variety of other clubs and activities. Samuel was on the board of the

National Honor Society, played the trumpet in the band, and served as a student body representative. Jacob was involved with the Mock Trial team, played the saxophone, and served on the board of the Associated Student Body group. Both boys were in Junior ROTC. Both were also active with the high school MEChA Club, the organization that dealt with issues of the Latino community. The phone seemed to ring constantly at the Sanchez household.

They wanted their home to be a special sanctuary, a safe place where they could be themselves, feel free from worldly judgments, and be shielded from the hectic pace of daily life. Spirituality and Bible study were important, and in addition to having daily readings from the Bible to start each day, Sunday mornings were held apart as special times for just the family.

Every Sunday during the boys' high school years, they unplugged the telephone, and for about an hour and a half the three sat at the kitchen table to talk. First, for ten minutes or so, they discussed selected Bible verses, relating the ideas to events in their lives and plans for the future. Then they would have a family meeting to talk over the mundane decisions that had to be made for the coming week: what events were on the calendar, who had to drive where, who should do what or should have done what. They also frequently spent Sunday evenings together. One family member was designated to rent an inspirational film from the local video store. A film about the courtmartial of an African American West Point cadet became a focus for extended conversation and reflection well beyond the Sanchez Sunday Night at the Movies.

Mapita envisions her home as a sanctuary, and she does not hesitate to take strong measures to keep it so. The telephone has no answering machine, and she does not hesitate to unplug it, even on days besides Sundays. Mapita also never feels compelled to answer the telephone if she is resting. She and the boys communicate well with their respective friends and colleagues in daily life, and they see their time at home as an opportunity to disconnect.

The concept of sanctuary does not hold just for their nuclear family. Visiting relatives are warmly embraced for as long as they can stay. A friend in need will be offered a bed for as long as may be required. One such guest was Daniel. He was the same age as the twins and had been kicked out of his own home by his father and stepmother. He was made to feel that he had a safe place to come to at the Sanchez home. The twins had known Daniel for many years.

Daniel became a good friend to the twins since they were all on the wrestling team. At home, however, he simply could not get along, and his backtalk and misdeeds earned him a variety of punishments from his parents, including orders to "mow" the entire front lawn with hand clippers. When Daniel packed his backpack and decided to live on his own, Jacob and Samuel pleaded his case at home with Mapita. They knew that Daniel could arrange to go live with his birth mother, so he'd need to stay with them for just a few weeks. She had a good feeling about Daniel, even though she knew that he could be difficult. And so, once Daniel knew that he was truly welcome by Mapita, Samuel, and Jacob, he relaxed. He was polite and helpful, and Mapita even agreed that if he needed to stay long enough to graduate and then travel across the country to his mother's, that would be all right.

Slow down to turn inward.

13. Love others as you love yourself; accept uncertainty

Showing others the same concern you would desire for yourself is a concept that is common to all of the world's great religions. Being altruistic is not always easy. Breaking down distances and barriers is one of the ways that parents can model love for others.

Showing children that they are lovable is a gift that wise parents may give their children. Love does not have to be demonstrated as syrupy affection; nor does a parent need to become a sugar daddy or mommy, always giving things to the kids. Rather, the Tao is reflected in enjoyment, caring, and respect. Wise parents understand that the symbols of caring will be different for each child. Gifts of all sorts need to be matched to the recipient to be meaningful. And gifts don't have to be expensive to be thoughtful. Giving of oneself can be the most meaningful. Developing self-love is also critical for parents. Victims of low self-esteem may find it hard to reach out to others.

The wise parent also knows that days with active children seldom turn out exactly as planned. Commitment and decisions are important, but most family activities can seldom be "cast in concrete." The forces of individual personalities, interruptions and plans that are imposed from outside the family, and variations in your own feelings about how things should go make a difference in what really happens.

Respect your own individuality and be proud of being a parent. Learn that change will always be part of your regular routine.

One winter holiday was unusual for the Williams family. Instead of preparing for a typical Christmas celebration at home, the family decided to take a trip. Months in advance, they decided that there would be no fancy, expensive gifts for any of the individual members of the family. Instead of finding store-bought items, each person in the family would make something for the other three family members. The money usually spent on presents would be saved and dedicated to a trip to England. Lew and Margaret had traveled in Great Britain early in their marriage and vowed to go back, for it had been delightful. Flying out on Christmas Day brought the plane fare way down, and since the Williams family tradition was to celebrate and open gifts on Christmas Eve at home, that date wouldn't be a problem.

The presents were nothing fancy, but they were appreciated.

Cynthia made necklaces and painted pictures. Patrick wrote stories and drew cartoons. Margaret made tiny models, including a
model wine and cheese party for Lew. And Lew wrote a beautiful
story for his wife, the first that she'd ever received from him. It
brought tears to her eyes.

London was cold and rainy, complete with winds that blew
umbrellas inside out and drenching downpours that got everyone's feet soaked. The apartment that was first assigned to the
family had mirrored walls and ceilings along with cockroaches.
Furthermore, although everyone found England and London life
to be very interesting, no one was totally head over heels in love
with things British at that point.

However, in spite of some less-than-perfect qualities, it was a
wonderful holiday. Lew and Patrick took a sprung couch cushion
and a dead cockroach as evidence to the manager of the sprawling apartment house, who found a cleaner, more flowery, slightly
more spacious, place for the Williams family. The family cama-
raderie that grew from sharing the homemade gifts blossomed in
a new strange environment as they tried to figure out unusual
schedules and maps and get around in the challenging weather.
The family enjoyed reading about British historical events and
the guidebooks about things to do. Each family member got to
choose some activities. Cynthia chose the British Museum with
its Elgin marbles and archaeological treasures and an Italian
restaurant. Patrick chose a gigantic toy store, where he purchased a fake rubber arm, and the Tower of London, where he
puzzled over the various types and sizes of armor. Lew chose a
concert of classical music and a pub named after his beloved
Sherlock Holmes. And Margaret chose the double-decker bus
tour of the city and the National Gallery, which had huge rooms
and huge paintings that they'd all seen in books and that were
truly awe-inspiring. Although they'd planned to travel outside
London during their long week in England, they all agreed that
they would have to come back some other day to do that. There
was too much to do and see right there in London, riding around
in the Underground in a world very different from their own.

Trekking around town was fun, but just as memorable were the times back in the rented flat, with its view of city buildings, its strange footed bathtub, warm towel bars, pull-chain water closet, and various giant-floral wallpapers. The British TV shows were appealing, the meals that were put together from ingredients gathered in unusual markets were tasty, and the warm rooms tucked away from the dreary weather appealed to a family from the southwestern United States. New Year's Eve came early to London, and it was exhilarating to have the family together to see in the day.

Do not take yourself too seriously.

14. The way is subtle; respect and apply the past

Wise parents respect the past in their decisions. What is "old" is not necessarily outdated. Mothers and fathers refer to the experiences of ancestors in order to make life's transitions a comfortable process. Reflecting on the practices of the past can enrich thinking about what is appropriate to do in the present.

Help your children to learn about your family's religions, symbols, stories, histories, values, and languages. Have a grandparent share his or her life story to bring deeper understanding and appreciation of the lives of others.

When Dot and John had been married for a year, they planned a family trip to the Midwest to meet all the relatives on both sides of the family. They wanted their children to have some of the same experiences that each of them had enjoyed during their earlier lives.

The family started off from California in the station wagon and made Phoenix the first stop before they went on to the

Grand Canyon. Then they camped across the nation, stopping to stay with John's college roommate and his family in Chicago before going to his parents' house in southern Illinois.

One strong thread within their travels was tracing their dad's roots. John's earliest days were spent in the true heartland of the United States. He was raised on a farm, and his conservative family, in spite of being poor, had demonstrated daily that generosity and religion were of great importance to them. A focus on goodness permeated the way John was raised. His parents' home was a modest frame house surrounded by tall elm trees. All six of Grandpa Ray's and Grandma Pat's kids had been born at home. They were all, including John, baptized in the pond at the side of the property. They all shared rooms in the small home. Out back was an outhouse that was "extra" now but had been a real necessity for many years as the kids were growing. In spite of their simple life, the Singleton family was known for reaching out to others.

When John's family arrived, John's sister and brother-in-law, Martha and Larry, brought family members together for a reunion and several potlucks on their hog farm. Potluck meals were served, with many varieties of casseroles and salads to accompany the ham, followed by fruit shortcakes and pies. Then, after everyone had finished eating, two aunts would play the piano and organ while everyone gathered round and sang hymns for two hours or so, harmony full, with all the verses sung by heart.

On the way home the family drove through Texas and visited with John's mother's twin sister, Aunt Bea, and her big sister, Aunt Helen. The two great-aunts spent hours sharing recipes with the girls, passing on secrets for the best cookies and cakes and salads. John couldn't resist engaging in religious debates with his maiden aunts, both retired schoolteachers. He said to Dot as they finally drove home that he wanted to stir them up. Dot knew from later letters that they spent a long time praying for her new husband and his marriage after their visit.

When John had decided to become an engineer, he surprised

his parents, for they had encouraged him in a very different direction. They had seen his future in the ministry or in missionary work in some faraway part of the world. In fact, his religious upbringing has strongly influenced his life. The Singletons are active in their church and like to take time to help others. And when their children grew up, they carried on the family tradition of caring for others, either professionally or as volunteers.

Look to the old ways, for they will bring present understanding.

15. Be cautious, reserved, flexible, sincere, and honest

Wise parents think before acting and speaking to children, modeling the same courtesies that they extend to adults in polite society. They are calm about personal issues and relations but excited about things that are being discovered and learned. Wise parents can change speeds with the needs of the context, realizing that relationships don't come in one size to fit all children. Being "real" with children is important, for they are able to sense the phony and they resent inauthentic comments.

Some individuals believe that they were "born" parents because they were the eldest in a sibling group. They are used to telling others what to do and what not to do. However, the more "innocent"—that is, open—a parent can be, the more he or she can learn.

Do not hesitate to distinguish between right and wrong with your children, but remember that a discussion will give your sons and daughters more than a lecture on your part. Be truthful with your children. Always avoid one-sided recollections of events, empty threats, false promises, and insincere compliments.

When Samuel and Jacob were in junior high, they were good

about resisting many temptations. Still, on several occasions, when they were only in seventh grade, they found themselves driving a car. Mapita's former brother-in-law was in the construction business and worked at several nearby projects. Because he really enjoyed the twins, he would invite them to come to various construction sites with him. As he knew, roaring across a construction site in a dump truck or pickup truck was a very attractive activity to the adolescents. "Hop in, Samuel," was too good an invitation to turn down.

Mapita didn't agree with Uncle Frank on a lot of things. His ways, including coarse language, were often intended to teach the boys to be "macho men." He was the sort of guy who would hand out twenty-dollar bills to please her boys and let them do whatever they liked at his house. He was a sincere, good man in many ways, who demonstrated overblown pride in being Italian and often made fun of Mexicans. Knowing what reckless attributes he possessed, she wasn't surprised to find out that her twelve-year-old sons were spending time driving around at Uncle Frank's work sites. She was not happy. Frank would respond, "Lighten up, Mapita. They're not going to die."

Mapita found out about the whole situation when she saw Samuel parking a truck at one site while she was driving home from work. Rather than launch into a burst of criticism, however, she spoke quietly to her son. He still remembers that she treated him like an adult and talked through the situation. She asked him to share what he thought were the possible dangers. Samuel assured his mother that she didn't have to worry, but he also explained what fears he had had. Within their conversation, Mapita also recalled an incident from the newspaper where a forklift operator had tipped over and been killed at a muddy construction site. When all was said and done, Samuel was the one to explain what would happen next. He agreed that he would tell his uncle that he could only help with some of the chores. No more driving until he got his license.

A still puddle becomes clear.

16. Know your background to connect with others

Wise parents learn about their own roots and share their reflection on the past. Although returning to the homeland of our ancient ancestors may not always be possible, discovering the ways in which the cultures of long-ago places and times affect the present can be inspiring and enriching. Personal recent heritage and present family cultural perspectives always affect the tone and content of what parents say, when and how they do things, and the things they give attention and the things they ignore.

Take the time to explore your own heritage by questioning others and using the computer searches now available. Write or tape your autobiography. Never hesitate to add to it, and always think about the impact your experiences have had on your understanding of life. You could start by describing something simple. Perhaps draw a map and describe where you played as a young child. Even the simplest piece will be a treasure to share with other relatives as well as with your children.

Kate and Carl have enjoyed selecting ideals and cultural traditions to uphold in their family life. The characteristics and activities that are special to them come from the best of two cultures. Kate's family carried on customs that stemmed originally from her mother's family, treasured traditions from Mexican culture. As a senior about to graduate, Holly wrote about her great-grandmother in the context of discussing Robert Frost's words, "Two roads diverged in a yellow wood":

> The year was 1901 and a young woman named Francisca Armendariz faced a similar situation, arriving at a crossroads that would impact generations to come. The first path continued with certainty in her native Mexico amidst family and friends.

The other turned sharply and harbored an intense amount of undergrowth so that she could hardly distinguish her future in a foreign land whose language she did not understand.

Nevertheless, this brave soul opted for the road that wanted wear and yearned for the tread of her cautious feet. Thus my great-grandmother crossed the Mexican border with the shelter of a covered wagon into the United States, the very day President McKinley was assassinated.

Kate's earliest memories from childhood go back to her grandparents' house on Greenwood Street, just one street over from Carl and Kate's current one-story frame house. She was always known as Katie in those days. Her grandmother was always known as Mamachita, and grandfather was always Papa Au, for reasons that were never fully explained to the grandchildren. Their house was a sprawling frame house at the end of the block, surrounded by fruit trees of many different kinds—figs, guavas, kumquats, loquats, oranges, and sapote. There they raised twelve children— seven sons and five daughters. Those children, Kate's mother and aunts and uncles, always returned as adults, often every day, to cook and visit and help their parents. The door was never locked. The house was never empty. It was a center for the family for over five decades.

Of the five sisters, Kate's mom, Carmella, was the only one who ever worked outside the home. Her husband had become quite ill when Kate and her sisters and brother were young. Carmella knew that her parents' home could offer a safe harbor for the children each day before they went to school, when they came home for lunch, and after they came home from school. Several of the aunts and uncles were always there. Uncle Pete worked as a doctor nearby. Uncle Albert was an architect. Uncle John had a printing business in the next town. Aunts Celia and Martha worked at home.

Lunchtime at Mamachita's and Papa Au's was always a big event and was well attended by family members. The menu *never* varied: homemade tortillas, lamb chops, beans, chili, and rice. Every single day. That was how Papa Au wanted it, and everyone thought that was just fine. It tasted delicious and pleased everyone.

Everybody was close in the Gonzalez family. Every Saturday morning, one of the uncles would drive from home to home to pick up all the cousins from their respective houses in the neighborhood or farther away. The kids spent the whole morning working in their grandparents' orchard. The older cousins got to sweep the dirt around the trees, working their brooms windmill-style to keep the ground neat. The younger cousins had the jobs of picking up dead fruit and getting things tidy around the house. Inside the house, Grandmother would sit on a stool for long stretches, peeling New Mexico chilies.

There was always great respect for the elders, and the frequent family celebrations and gatherings were considered to be very important. On Christmas Eve, everyone in the extended family would gather for Santa Claus to come and bring gifts to all the children. Each child was made to feel very special as Santa called his or her name, handing a colorfully wrapped package into the waiting hands. The aunts brought out trays of tamales that they had prepared many days ahead of time. Traditional American Christmas songs were the main entertainment, from *The Twelve Days of Christmas* to *Silent Night*. After midnight, everyone would go to their own homes, having spent the holiday with at least ninety-nine of their local relatives.

Now, even though Mamachita and Papa Au have passed on, the stories and certain values continue to prevail, even though the number of family members has gotten smaller as families have gotten smaller. Holly and Corey have lived through it all, although much of their experience has been vicarious. They have come to understand many of the values that their family holds dear, and they have seen how they overlap and intersect with the beliefs of many other groups of people. They may be different in how they honor a certain value, but not in holding the value itself. A Santa Party still always takes place on Christmas Eve. It isn't at the old family home, though. Instead, family members travel by air to get together at one of Kate's sisters' houses in northern California. Kate's twin sisters, Carmella and Patti, get together and throw a gigantic party for their families and close friends. The elders are still honored, and all the children and grandchildren are *very* attentive to the needs of Kate's mom, who is now in a wheelchair since her stroke. At any family gathering it would be typical to see one of the grandchildren sitting and chatting for a long time by Grandma Carmella's chair. Senora Carmella lives near Tina, Kate's older sister, and other family members visit her many times a week.

Customs go on, altered by each family and generation, but perpetuated through stories that get told over and over and by family pictures that get shown over and over. Kate believes in saving treasured memories by hanging special pictures on the wall, stashing the rest of the pictures in a special saving bag to *really* get organized some day, and keeping family stories and traditions alive by telling them—or about them—again and again.

Explore your own story to understand others.

17. Have faith in others so they will have faith in you

Faith does not survive where there is criticism, suspicion, fear . . . or ignorance. When parents treat children with respect, the ways children treat their parents in return can be respectful and gratifying. The parent-child relationship in the Tao promotes doing activities together as opposed to having the parent play the role of primary giver and doer. When parents learn about the personal interests and activities of their children, they can interweave their knowledge with the choices that are made for family life and activities.

Have faith in your children's responsibility for living and growing. It will allow them to fulfill your expectations.

Cynthia had some difficult times as a teenager. Her struggles surprised Margaret, who had had a much easier time of growing up. How could it be so hard, when this talented daughter had so much more "on the ball" than she'd ever had? Margaret realized that when she was a teenager, her plans were to some day get married and have four children. In her framework for life, a job was simply something to do during those few years between college and marriage; plans for a lifetime career were at that time still mostly for men. As it turned out, life became much more complex, full of responsibilities and twists and turns, both personal and professional, but Margaret faced decisions as they arose; they did not loom constantly ahead during her youth.

Cynthia, on the other hand, was searching to identify the right choices to make for college, lifestyle, and a career ahead. Unlike her mother, she was entering adulthood at a time when women were expected to be *everything*: talented career woman, marvelous wife, caring mother, and a socially "with it" person at the same time. It was not easy. Many women could attest to that.

Margaret realized that in her eagerness to expose Cynthia to the many cultural opportunities she herself enjoyed, she had not taken time to appreciate the music, the foods, the television shows, and the activities that her daughter liked. She decided that she needed to pay attention to the forces that were really present in her daughter's life. When she finally decided to devote time to the process, there were many surprises—some good, some not so good.

Going to Marlborough Street was one part of the education. Although Cynthia had gone there many times with friends, Margaret had only heard about this place. The street was filled with young people who dressed in thick-soled boots, oversized jeans, undersized dresses, thick makeup, and spiked hairstyles streaked with magenta or chartreuse. The clerks in the stores were similar in their dress and appearance. But Margaret was surprised to find the clerks were well-spoken and polite.

The goods in the various stores were also strange to her tastes. Skimpy polyester dresses (Where are the wool and cotton?), mostly in black (Where are the flattering colors?), water pipes and smoking gear (Haven't they accepted that smoking is bad for you?), and shops with tattoos (Their skin is decorated for life!) and piercing rings (Whatever for? Ouch!) and with loud music blasting (Where was Mozart when you needed him?).

When they ate a lunch of coffee and bagel sandwiches, Margaret felt on familiar ground once again. Cynthia exclaimed, "Isn't this great?" and Margaret replied, "Yes. I'm glad I came," not because she could change her feelings about the strange things around her, but because she could now understand why her daughter cared about such things. The environment was interesting and invigorating, festive and friendly. It reminded her of visits to the central city she'd made as a teenager.

Listening to tapes and CDs of Cynthia's favorite groups was another experience. After too many years of hearing music behind Cynthia's bedroom door (Please turn that down!) or thumping gently out of her Walkman, Margaret took the plunge and spent some time truly listening to music, with Cynthia and on her own, and learned that there were many nuances to it that she'd never had the time to appreciate.

Reading a book about tattoos was another eye-opener. The beautiful photographs showed the artistic side of this phenomenon, taking it out of the sailors-and-honky-tonk perspective she'd grown up with. Cynthia said, "Mom, why don't you get one?" And Margaret replied, "Well, if I did, I think I'd want a lily of the valley. But I won't. You'll love me just the same."

Believe in one another.

18. When the way is not followed or family relationships are not in harmony, hypocrisy and pious advocates arise

In the Tao, good choices are made within the family. Decisions are not made by forces outside the family. When familial harmony is threatened or lost, outsiders' practices and activities can become influential, but they can be inappropriate and deleterious to the Tao.

Only outsiders who help you to reflect and make your own decisions will make a difference in the long run. The voices of outside "experts" who tell you what to do can confuse the issues at hand.

Follow your own sensibility when others tell you what to do. You will find the way.

John's former wife Nancy—and her/his children—felt it would be a good idea to celebrate Christmas together as a large, extended family. They'd had several get-togethers and couldn't see why Christmas would be any different. John, in his easygoing way, and Dot, wanting to please others as was her way, tried it out. They attended a large Christmas gathering at Polly's house one year, and because it was an open house, it worked all right. Still, the atmosphere was tense. Although John's children were anxious to have the family gather as "one big happy family" and include Nancy in their family trips, Dot and John found this arrangement uncomfortable. So Nancy is not included in their regular get-togethers. The children weren't pleased by this, but John and Dot have stuck to it.

John and Dot decided that birth parents and stepparents should attend major events, like graduations and weddings. John holds telephone conversations with Nancy about key issues and money matters, and she has managed to thank him for being a good father.

Dot's former husband, on the other hand, has been in and out of alcohol rehabilitation and has had three more marriages since his first. He remains in the shadows as far as his children's lives are concerned. Dot thinks that the distance is not for the best, but she prefers it to the strange closeness that was imposed upon her as a child. Her own mother and stepdad were subjected to surprise visits when Dot's real father, Martin, would just show up with his family, even for extended stays of two weeks at a time. Dot knew later, when she was a parent experiencing the same thing, that her parents were incredibly gracious to allow this so that the two girls, Dot and her sister, could get to know their "real" father. Furthermore, although it had felt good to know her father, it seemed, when she was an adult with similar circumstances to deal with, that it was going overboard to have to relate for long stretches of time.

Seek information from the source—your inner self. Deterioration follows when personal relations become false-hearted.

19. Reduce selfishness; have few desires

In the Tao, parents don't hire a circus when a storybook will do. Some people fall into the trap of always wanting more. As soon as one wish is fulfilled, others rush to be accommodated. Fathers and mothers often take on additional jobs to purchase those "little extras" for their families. As they add layers of possessions to their lives, they inadvertently detract from the core of family life. Without time together, family life becomes hollow.

As wise parents, do not drain your fiscal and physical resources in order to find "happiness."

Dot is the designated money manager for her family, and she admits, "I don't know much about money, but I just figure out how to purchase the things that we need or earn money to pay for the activities that we decide to do. Money is merely a tool, not something unto itself. We want to enjoy life and each other, and somehow, we seem to have little miracles along the way. None of us is afraid to work hard when it is necessary."

When the children were young, and Dot and John's marriage was new, the family car was the "Green Mean Machine," a used Ford station wagon that was purchased inexpensively and ran around under a coat of putrid green paint. Everyone agreed that it was ugly, but it served its intended function well, taking five kids and their friends to the beach or the park or the nature trail. Dot wanted to get to know her kids—all of them—and she felt that she needed a big car to spend time with them. Along the way, other vehicles were selected for the ways they could serve the family and stay up and running, definitely not for their status. The children never seemed to complain about the assortment of old trucks, a used camper trailer, and off-road vehicles because they provided many opportunities for fun together.

Dot and John believe in giving their children *experiences*, not money, and not things. The purchase of a rustic cabin in the remote mountains of Utah was designed to give the family time away from their busy lives to be together, enjoying the woods, playing in the snow, and skiing at the cabin. These trips required cooperation and working together to travel to the isolated location and to heat the cabin with logs and keep it in good order. From the first, friends were always welcome. To John and Dot, building memories of chopping wood together is more important than playing video games alone. Such simple activities gave the family time to grow closer and express their warmth for each other without expensive gadgets or elaborate vacations.

Manifest plainness, embrace simplicity. These are the ways to seek wealth in experience.

20. Do not see things in black and white

Seeking to understand circumstances can be illuminating. Behaviors and values that appear clearcut in one setting may lose their importance in another. It is important to look at others outside the family with caring. In the Tao, parents also learn to accept one another even though their backgrounds may yield very different ideas and practices. One parent's prohibition may be another parent's pleasure; one parent's rudeness may just be assertiveness to another. Parents need to work out their differences and provide a partnership that may not always present a perfectly united front but does demonstrate the ways in which individuals can respect one another and agree to disagree within a range of options. As a unit, each family must examine beliefs and establish its own guidelines about issues such as schoolwork and behavior. Details can be changed as the needs of family members change, but the framework can remain.

Learn to suspend judgment and see actions and events as part of a context. Look at the big picture—and at the long picture that includes the future—before you make decisions.

Margaret and Lew are pretty easygoing. They both think, however, that being flexible doesn't mean shirking responsibility or neglecting promises. When Cynthia and Patrick were in elementary school, they both joined scout troops. Cynthia was a Brownie, then a Junior, and then a Girl Scout. Patrick was first a Tiger, then a Cub Scout, and then a Webelo Scout.

Although the Williams parents both had full-time jobs, they took on the leadership of the boys' troop on two occasions, and they helped out in other years, driving to campouts and helping with various troop activities, including holding many meetings at their home during the year that Cynthia was in a "cooperative" girl scout troop. They did this to make sure that the group had leaders, since other parents were not jumping at the opportunity.

More important, the leadership opportunities gave them a chance to know other kids the same age as their child. It was re-assuring to find that some behaviors aren't all that unusual when you see eight other eight-year-olds or ten-year-olds doing the same thing. Margaret and Lew enjoyed meeting the other parents. They formed longstanding friendships with adults in their neighborhood. It was also a chance to see how each child would express himself or herself in various settings.

When Patrick was beginning to learn outdoor skills in scout-ing, and the time came to have a practice campout, it turned out that getting a trip together was beyond everyone's resources that spring. So the campout was held in the Williams's family's back yard. The boys set up their tents on the lawn by the vegetable garden, and they prepared their meals on the picnic table on the patio. They roasted marshmallows and hot dogs on the coals over the charcoal cooker that was lowered to campfire height on the driveway. The house was for bathroom privileges only. An ideal overnight? Not exactly. Patrick turned into a goof-off, a mini-monster, right before his parents' eyes.

The well-mannered son who seldom needed correction at school and was pretty cooperative at regular scout meetings, was, at home, a scout troop terror, erupting with rude noises, ig-noring directions, making smart remarks and showing off at every turn. Luckily, there were two leaders—Lew and Margaret had each other. They agreed not to be harsh but rather to take Patrick aside and remind him of his usual thoughtfulness and his typical politeness, and set these expectations over again. It took more than one consultation. Reflecting on the episode later, Mar-garet and Lew agreed that firm but kind handling was the only way that could have worked. Luckily, since they knew their son in many different settings, they knew that he wasn't a bad boy, though the acts and attitudes for the context were pretty awful. They also realized that the same principles applied to the other boys in the group.

Parenting life is full of difficult decisions, and most of them are not guided by clear rules. Lew and Margaret declare that many things that seem "wrong" to them are not bad in and of themselves. Some things would be just fine . . . for someone else's children. When Cynthia announced for the first time that she wanted to get a tattoo, she was fifteen. Lew and Margaret said no. It was a decision with implications for the rest of her life. It would be painful and costly to remove if she didn't like it. Take time to think about it, they told her. When she turned eighteen, she could do as she chose.

Over time, Cynthia shared her thoughts about various designs and what she'd like to have for her tattoos. Margaret remembered that she had been raised in an era when schoolgirls didn't do such things. Sailors, carnival workers, and motorcyclists did, but not middle-class teenage girls. She thought that as Cynthia matured, she would see that a tattoo might not fit into the longer picture for herself. But times have changed. Around the time of her eighteenth birthday, Cynthia came home with a small sun pictured on her ankle. It was a real tattoo all right. Permanent, kind of cute, and only the first.

The distance between no and yes is not great in the dictionary of life.

21. The way is real, but elusive; intuition leads

The Tao does not always deal with measurable, observable phenomena. The best thing for a parent to do in a given day may not be the next thing in an externally determined sequence. Just as "real" scientists do not get their ideas and achieve their findings through the structured perfection of the steps in the scientific method, parents do not gain understanding through clearcut connections. Knowledge is gained in much more personal ways, through intuition and experience. Hunches that lead to seemingly appropriate decisions may be supported in retrospect by empirical information.

Learn to trust your own feelings and encourage activities, such as brainstorming, that allow personal insights to be respected. What "feels" right to do may be the very best thing to do. Understand that what is practical for today may be disastrous for life.

Mapita doesn't want her sons to be "Mama's boys," but she is ever-conscious of circumstances for their safety. Living in a town where gang activity is well known and several drive-by shootings are documented, she thinks twice about what she lets her sons do. During high school, when Halloween was approaching, Samuel wanted to join his friends at the "Scary Night" events at the amusement park in the next city. He wanted to drive over, meet his friends, and drive home at two in the morning. He was obviously old enough to take care of himself, he insisted. Still, Mapita simply did not feel right about the situation. Her older sister, Karina, was visiting, and Aunt Karina felt free to enter into the discussion. She thought they should stay home. The whole event sounded too dangerous to her. But Aunt Karina lived in a different town and came from an era even more distant than Mapita, and she had little knowledge about the annual event and its positive reputation for safety. No, keeping her son home wasn't what went through Mapita's mind. Yes, he could probably go to the Scary Night. Yes, she knew that the boys had driven around town safely many, many times. But, no, this wasn't something that he should drive himself to. Yes, he was a careful, expert driver. Yes, he was a good kid. Yes, he would avoid well-known dangerous areas as he drove across two cities. But in the end, no, he couldn't go unless he was willing to have her drive him and pick him up. Why she made her decision wasn't based exactly on the facts. The boys wanted her to change her mind, but by then her mind was made up. She knew. And the boys knew she knew, even though there wasn't a perfect reason that any of them could explicitly identify. And, as in many other decision-making situations, her "gut feelings" had to prevail.

So, in spite of the fact that staying up until 2:00 A.M. wasn't *her* favorite thing to do, Mapita drove the boys there and brought them home, and they were safe and sound.

On the other hand, intuition led Mapita to go against her own, strong anti-gun, antiwar beliefs to allow her sons to join the high school junior ROTC. A military lifestyle was certainly alien to her, but the man who led the local high school group was a good person with a reputation for fairness and thoughtfulness. Her feeling for the situation was positive, even in spite of her past experiences and values. It felt right. As time went by, Mapita saw benefits that came with the boys' membership. They had leadership opportunities that required careful decision making. They made new friends and became physically fit. And, most important to her, they understood the importance of serving their community.

What seemed just as strange to her at first was the fact that her sons wanted to become wrestlers when they got to high school. Why not swimming? Why not running? Cross-country would be so much better for them! Track meets didn't require possibly hurting anyone. How could her peaceful children engage in a sport that expected competition and physically interfering with others?

But wrestling became a way of life, not only for the boys, but for their mama as well. Attending meets, eating carefully to keep within weight limits, and keeping daily and weekly schedules that centered around practices and meets became a way of life for many months each year, with Mapita sitting in the bleachers to be there for the boys.

The Way is mysterious, but its essence can reveal high moral cultivation.

22. Teach by example

The power of "showing how it's done" has been demonstrated over and over in many settings. In the home, the examples that parents set are close and constant.

Most often, a parent's example becomes a model and children follow in the footsteps of their mothers and fathers. Examples certainly can teach what not to do, and teens are usually the ones who most often recognize that fact in their thoughts and words: "I will never do that when I'm a parent!" All too often, though, those become "famous last words" as their life progresses into new stages, and they become the parents.

Example, through words and deeds, can do it all. Keep an ear and an eye on your deeds and words.

Holly and Corey see their mom and dad as good examples in the way they have set priorities over time and made sacrifices for their family and for their children.

Fatherhood is a pleasure for Carl. He has been an important influence in the lives of both his daughter and his son . . . for different reasons. As Kate puts it, Holly was able to form much of her sense of personhood from her father. She never thought of herself as having boundaries in terms of ability. Carl gave her lots of time and encouragement, whether it was working on a funny caricature or struggling with a math problem. Dad and daughter shared the enjoyment of listening to the blues—collecting tapes and attending concerts. Holly always knew that she could travel far and come home to a safe harbor.

Carl was always there for Corey when he got involved in sports, encouraging him from the sidelines. Although Carl himself was never very involved with playing in sports, he learned about the finer points of football and became quite a fan when his son chose that sport as his passion. His dad knew when and what to compliment as well as the best of fans.

Carl always encouraged Corey to be whatever he wanted to be, but he also showed him that dads could take on many responsibilities in the home. Father, and then son, enjoyed cooking a lot. Corey was often the one to start dinner cooking before his parents got home from work. In addition, he would often treat his friends to a great breakfast when they came to spend a night at his house . . . bacon, eggs, pancakes, waffles, hash browns . . . the works. And, like his dad, he would even notice when Kate was about to burn the cookies, and he would rescue them from the oven when she got involved on the phone.

Don't try to impress. The real you will shine forth.

23. Use few words

Parents certainly have words that are important for their children to hear, but they must choose them carefully and use them sparingly—to attract children to ideas, to encourage them to go on, to direct them in positive ways. In a discussion, the wise parent knows that the communication is two-way; it is necessary for the child to speak or respond before the parent speaks again. In the Tao, the parent who practices the art of listening will be successful. Children come to know that they are important and credible when conversations are not regularly turned into lectures.

Set aside regular times to be with your children. Plan to have meals with the family and do other activities together. Use evocative words and subtle questions, calling forth the children's ideas, not yours, and show pleasure at their ideas and solutions to problems.

Kate has learned to "back off" over the years. Some ways of talking simply don't work. At least, not with Corey. When she was on a kick to get her son to become a voracious reader and strong student, she constantly admonished him. "Put the newspaper away. Don't you have a test tomorrow? Do you have homework? Quit stalling. Have you been watching TV? Isn't there a long-term project you need to do? Do you have at least a B in every class? How much do you have to do?" Kate eventually realized that all that harping didn't make a bit of difference.

Carl always says far less, and waits to speak, but it always tends to carry more weight. He has been known to say, "This is your most important semester. Are you getting at least a B in every class?" Even though he tends to say the same thing each semester, it gets a response from Corey.

Seeing things in a different light has not been easy for Carl and Kate. They have made a pact not to compare Corey's easygoing academic habits to the precise and eager ways that were typical of Holly. They now can appreciate many of the things that Corey really does do well; they have watched him develop many admirable qualities without overt instruction from them.

Corey actually does a great amount of reading. He devours the newspaper sports pages daily, and he reads every school newsletter and newspaper. If a magazine has sports in it, he will read it avidly. Corey is a very punctual person, just like his parents. He's also quite dedicated to attending school, with years of perfect attendance.

Corey is easygoing and has a lot of friends. He enjoys dancing, and although he claims that he could *never* be as crazy a dancer as his mother, he is always willing to get out on a dance floor. He is also great with little kids. Not only is he attentive to his younger cousins, but he enjoys visiting the elementary school. The kindergarten kids are thrilled to death on the day he comes to help and play.

Some things have rubbed off on Corey from his parents, and his sister, without anyone telling him to do them. He has grown to love exercise, although he isn't as eager to get up at five in the morning to work out as his parents. He is also a big animal lover, and he's good at getting other people to be nice to animals. He's been known to say things like: "How would you like to be a dog?" and "Feed the dog before you feed yourself."

According to the kids, the reading aloud that both parents did during their early childhood years was really very important—far more than any straight talk that might have occurred. Whether it was Mom reading *Good Night, Moon, The Little Engine That Could*, or the Frog and Toad books, or Dad reading *Charlie and the Chocolate Factory* or *James and the Giant Peach*, the experience was warm, and the messages were special.

Kate sometimes wishes that her words could change things. It seems so easy—I'll tell you what to do and you'll do it. Instead, she calls on her patience; the time needed for words to soak in and behaviors to rub off is, as she has learned, often rather long.

Think before you speak; ration your own words. It is Nature's way to say little.

24. Progress is slow; do not boast

Human growth and learning are often evolutionary in nature. Gradual development over time is the rule, although leaps do occur. When our children develop, they are expressing the codes that have been transmitted to them through their unique genetic compositions. When development proceeds rapidly or well, parents are proud and sometimes get the feeling that they are the cause of their child's advanced ways. Rapid progress can make parents boast. However, the wise parent does not engage in self-promotion. It tends to be a sign of an insecure person.

On the other hand, some children may grow and develop at a very slow rate. In spite of knowing better, the mother or father may feel that he or she is to blame. The parent who spends a great deal of time worrying about a child's progress is using valuable time that might better be spent in more meaningful activities.

See your children as individuals who will move through stages of growth in their own special ways. Your sons and daughters, especially as adolescents, will see a wide variety of developmental phases in their classmates at school. Help each child to understand and appreciate that he or she is unique and, at the same time, "normal."

Polly Singleton was a bright student all through school, but at the same time she was headstrong in social situations. So it was in junior high. Unfortunately, she didn't want to follow the rules of the public junior high school, and she couldn't stand rushing from class to class, meeting the demands of half a dozen different teachers. She always spoke her mind, and teachers came to dread their encounters with her. After a disastrous first quarter, she decided to transfer to a public school with an alternative program, where she stayed through ninth grade.

When the time came to make decisions about high school, there was no doubt in anyone's mind that the alternative school would be a good choice for Polly. It was a public school, but it had many features that made it seem like a private school. The school was more flexible, and the faculty took a great deal of personal interest in the students. It provided a safe and stimulating haven for Polly. Each day began with a meeting with a "family" group of a teacher and eight or nine other students. Desks weren't the prominent features of classrooms. Instead, project work took place at tables, and couches were available in many places for reading and talking. The individualized program allowed students to select courses each quarter, and Polly was able to select several courses in the arts and in photography, capitalizing on her strengths. All in all, the unusual school was good for her, and she graduated as an award winner in her class.

At the same time, however, Polly had difficulties with other aspects of her life. She didn't like rules, since her birth mother's strong philosophy had been quite laissez faire. Polly had been raised in that sort of environment for most of her years. In addition, she didn't hesitate to speak bluntly to anyone who attempted to exert authority over her. Dot's presence in her family life meant that she was expected to meet one more person's expectations. She refused to acquiesce, and her blunt talk and defiant actions were unsettling for Dot. At one point, in only one of many blowups, Dot was attempting to discuss birth control with her stepdaughter, who was spending a great deal of time with a male admirer. Polly exclaimed loudly that she was *not* a slut. Dot was crushed at the way her comments had been taken. Nevertheless, they were convinced that Polly was going to grow in her relationship skills with time.

To better understand their roles, John and Dot went to counseling sessions for stepparents and determined that they needed to come back to Polly with their parental boundaries clarified. Then the decision to accept or reject those boundaries was Polly's. Ultimately, her decision was rejection, and that meant moving out, which she did. Dot and John established that as long as she lived with a friend (not a boyfriend) she would keep her financial support for school. She attended two years of community college, two more years of college and got a master's degree in medical social work and then had a career as a successful broker. It took time for Polly to mature and find her niche, but she did.

Encourage your children and do not claim their successes as your own.

25. History repeats itself

Wise parents know that, in spite of the powerful effects of current social trends, fashions, and political forces, certain family qualities do persist over time. Not that we must stick to the old adages, "Like father, like son," or "The acorn seldom falls far from the tree." We know that a variety of forces such as education, social class, ethnic groups, geographic location, and friendships interact in complex ways. Still, when historians, biologists, anthropologists, and sociologists study generations of families, they note that many sets of traits remain consistent, some because of nature (genes) and some because of nurture (factors in the environment).

Many genetic influences were never suspected before the advances of modern research. Studies of grown twins, especially those who were separated at birth and raised as single children, show that they often act and interact as adults in ways that are amazingly similar. When parents mature, they (or those around them) see how they have become replicas of their own parents in many physical, psychological, and intellectual ways. Sometimes the effect is negative. (Help, I'm becoming my mother!) Sometimes it is positive. (I guess I got some of Dad's artistic talent after all.)

The ways in which generations express shared values and modeled ways of living are also powerful. Quite often, individuals criticize their parents or their children for qualities that are prominent in their own behaviors (but perhaps not within their self-awareness). On a different note, parents who care to remember may hear echoes of their own parents' words when they see how their past behaviors as children are reflected in their children's ways. "Just wait until you have children of your own," and "I hope you have a daughter just like you," are comments that gain clarity with time.

Pay attention, learning to identify negative family attributes as shared problems, and rejoice in the traits you have that provide joy in life.

Lew and Margaret were amused when friends commented on the birth of their first child. Some friends and acquaintances told Lew, "Cynthia looks just like *you*!" Others told Margaret, "She looks *just* like you!" Similar comments occurred five years later when Patrick was born. Margaret and Lew noticed, as time went on, that some years Cynthia *did* look a lot like her father and less like her mother, and vice versa. Patrick looked like his mom at birth and then not again until late in his elementary school years. As the children matured, other family resemblances were frequently noted.

Cynthia's parents were perplexed when she entered eighth grade and began to retreat to her bedroom and shut the door rather than spend time with them. She was distant in ways that she'd never been as a younger girl. She would leap up from the dinner table as soon as she'd eaten her food and act short or snappish when Margaret or Lew made any inquiries or requests. Telephone calls became long, private matters. "Close the door, please. Hang up the other phone. Don't worry about it, this is *my* room." As Lew and Margaret talked with one another about the circumstances, they agreed that it *was* her room and she did have the right to privacy. Still, her constant distance wasn't comfortable.

It wasn't until they remembered their own adolescent years that Margeret and Lew started to gain new perspective on their child's situation. As adolescents, each of them had had a strong need to go off on their own. Lew remembered spending long hours away from home, even hanging out with freight train hobos down at the railroad yards in his town. Margaret remembered long private hours at home reading books and crying over the characters' plights, and spending other long hours alone exploring the local fields and climbing trees to sit and sway in the branches. The times were new, the context was different, but the same sorts of behaviors were there. They decided that it wouldn't do any good to criticize Cynthia. They even told her stories about what it was like when they were her age and not such gregarious individuals either. Their standards for *some* family dinners and spending *some* time together didn't change, but they relaxed.

Contemplate the circle of the Tao. Your children will follow in your footsteps.

26. Take your time; be attentive and receptive

A wise parent learns to be a good listener. Empathy can only come from truly hearing and understanding what your child thinks. Listening does not imply agreement, nor does it necessitate a response. Very often, when your children have shared their concerns with you, and when they have seen your attentive gaze, your nodding head, and your sympathetic expression, they can go on to do the job or solve the problem themselves.

Parents in the Tao may find it valuable to take the time to write down (or even tape-record) what their children say and reflect on the words at a later time. They may be surprised at what they have missed in one hearing. Few words are necessary when others listen well, and if they are really listened to, children will learn that, as time goes on, they need parent comments less and less. They will become increasingly less dependent on parents' approval and rely more on their own.

Join the children on their wavelengths. You can demonstrate your acceptance of who each child is by your willingness to give of yourself. Be receptive. Know yourself and help your children to know you. Don't let shifts in emotion (anger, joy, sorrow) shroud who you really are.

When Jacob and Samuel and Mapita have a discussion, the conversation is full of everyone's impressions, not just the mother's. When the boys have something to say, Mapita listens to them. She does not always agree, but she treats their ideas with respect. The boys know that she always waits to hear the whole story and that she doesn't take sides until she knows as much as she can. She is open-minded.

After listening with care to Samuel and Jacob tell the story behind Samuel's unfair grade of D in Ms. Monzon's history class, Mapita knew that she would have to pay a visit to the school. She also decided that she would avoid a lot of possible "He said . . . she said . . ." sidetracking if she made sure her son came with her to talk to his teacher. Any misconceptions could be cleared up right then and there. The problem, as he had explained it very carefully at home, was that he had really earned a B in the class, but he'd had some work time to make up. Ms. Monzon had a very elaborate point system in her class, where students could earn and lose hundreds of points at a time. He had lost two hundred of his four hundred points because he hadn't gone to a proper after-school detention session. Because he had obligatory wrestling practices during every proposed after-school time, Jacob had taken it upon himself to check in at the Saturday study hall session instead. The teacher who was proctoring the Saturday hours assured Jacob that he would deliver the explanatory note to Ms. Monzon on Monday, and he did. However, she was furious that the teenager had taken it upon himself to go on Saturday instead of the weekday. She insisted that the penalty had to be paid in an afternoon study hall under *her* supervision.

When Jacob stuck to his argument that he had fulfilled *his* side of the bargain, his teacher said he had not. Jacob, however, reminded her that they had both signed a contract when the consequence was first designed. At the conference, Ms. Monzon wouldn't get the paper out at first. She first claimed there was no paper. Then she said she would have no idea where such a paper might be. But Mapita said, quietly but firmly, "We should look at the contract." When the paper was finally laid out on the desk before them, the answer was clear. Both teacher and student had, indeed, signed an official agreement: Jacob was supposed to fulfill four hours of detention—no mention of place, no mention of day.

At another time, in another incident, Samuel's teacher prescribed Saturday school for him because he had left class twenty minutes early in order to go to the gym to prepare for a wrestling trip to another school. Although Jacob's teacher had told him simply to come in before school and get the work he missed in the twenty minutes, Samuel's teacher, Dr. Wolf (who was also the school's assistant principal), had required him to put in four hours of makeup time as a penalty. When Jacob saw Dr. Wolf out in the school quad, he went up to him and asked, "Don't you think that it seems unfair for my brother to pay such a big penalty? If he had ditched a *whole class* he would have the same penalty." Dr. Wolf snapped that it was none of Jacob's business and that *he* didn't have to explain *any*thing to *any* student.

Mapita listened to her son. Then she called the school and talked with Dr. Wolf. She had with her a copy of the high school discipline pamphlet that described what punishments were appropriate for various infractions of rules. Missing part of a class would result in a detention. Missing a whole class meant Saturday school. And the school's mission statement included a passage about keeping the lines of communication between students and school faculty and administration open. "Dr. Wolf, I'm reading from the policy section of your school brochure. Your school is committed to 'empower and prepare all students to acquire the knowledge and skills needed to become responsible, productive, lifelong learners.' You believe in 'mutual respect, honesty, integrity, caring, and creativity.' If a child ditches class, the first offense is a detention. I'm sure that you have looked at the policy. In addition, I'm not asking you to excuse him from the appropriate consequences. By the way, I am sorry that you don't understand our culture. Jacob was not being disrespectful. In my absence, my son believes that he needs to support his brother. That is our way." By the end of the conversation, it was clear to both parties that Mapita expected the school to keep its promises, and she promised that her sons would abide by the same principles.

Your children need you to listen . . . with care.

27. Discipline yourself before trying to discipline others

Parents must look closely at the things that they do. "Do as I say, not as I do" has been a hallmark of ineffective parenting for a long, long time. Parents may say wonderful, inspiring things now and then. However, they do the things that they do on a very regular basis. Parents who settle down in front of the television as they tell their child to go read a book should not wonder if their youngster doesn't read much. At the same time, demonstrating through example is effective only if what's being modeled is clear.

Reading promotes reading. Children become good readers in homes where parents read to them daily and where the parents are readers themselves. In the same fashion, children's television viewing can be most effectively monitored where parents are selective viewers and the TV is off more than it is on. Thrifty habits can be developed in families where purchases are discussed in terms of value for the money and stores are selected to provide good terms. Conservation of resources will be valued in a home where recycling occurs and water is not wasted. Orderliness and cleanliness are best promoted in a family where chores and routines support them.

Take the time to do those things that you expect from your children.

From the time Cynthia and Patrick were very small, Lew and Margaret took turns so that each night at least one parent was a bedtime reader. Sometimes both parents came in to say goodnight. Teeth got brushed, faces washed, kisses given, and for twenty or thirty minutes books got read or stories got told. Sometimes a lullaby or a song was part of the ritual as well. The times were fun, but it took commitment on both parents' parts for they were tired after long days at their respective jobs.

Lew often told stories from an ongoing set about characters he'd invented as he went along. Prominent in many of the episodes were Robin Redbreast and Mary Meadowlark, with guest appearances by Oliver Owl, Henry Hawk, Ricky Road-runner, and Carl Crow. The stories weren't very concise and they rambled a lot, but there was always a problem to solve or a moral to reaffirm. Lew always made mention of people and things that were unmistakably familiar to Patrick and Cynthia in their daily lives.

Here is part of one story that Lew told Cynthia. He told her many about the same cast of birds over time.

Robin flew over the girl's house; he saw her playing with her dolls. He saw her mother working on the potted plants in the driveway and, down the hill, a man with a big funny hat worked in his garden. Then Robin flew down past the houses and toward the big open field where his friend Mary Meadowlark lived. As he neared Mary's place, Robin saw a cloud of dust where tall golden grass and green bushes should have been. There was a red tractor moving through the field, tearing up the ground. Robin was scared. He knew they were not far from Mary's nest.

When it was Margaret's evening to tell a bedtime story, she'd stretch across the bed or sit with her back against the side of the bed, telling morality tales in which the main character was named Cynthia or Patrick. The heroes were enthusiastic about doing good deeds, nice to old people, great at saving hurt animals, quick to remedy mistakes that they had made, and swift to apologize for unintentional wrongs.

One day a little boy named Patrick was walking down the sidewalk with his friend when a lady with gray hair came toward them, pushing a silver-colored walker in front of her. Patrick was used to walkers because he often helped his grandmother. Gram had walked with a walker since before he was born. Patrick was really quite thoughtful . . .

Parents and children shared books even more often than made-up stories. Regular trips to the library kept the family well stocked with plenty of books. The children usually made the choices, both at the library and at home each evening, of the story to be read. Nevertheless, each parent would lobby for a favorite or two now and then. Some books were read over and over again when the children were very young. Over and over, Lew or Margaret read *The Hungry Caterpillar*, *The Little Engine That Could*, *The Tale of Peter Rabbit*, and Dr. Seuss books. Patrick's favorite books as a youngster included the Berenstain Bears books, *Where the Wild Things Are*, and books written and illustrated by Leo Politti or Steven Kellogg. Patrick *didn't* much care for Dr. Seuss the way Cynthia did, but he liked Chris Van Allsburg even better.

Later on, books with humor and twists like *Louis the Fish*, the Shel Silverstein books of poetry, and *The Apple* were popular. Mom and Dad enjoyed those every bit as much as their kids.

Margaret and Lew have always been grateful for the story times they spent with their children. The closeness of bedtime reading and storytelling was always special. The reading also helped their children to be early and enthusiastic readers. Their only regret is that when the children left the primary grades and read so very well themselves, they didn't continue the bedtime readings. Books by Roald Dahl, Mildred Taylor, or Judy Blume would have been great to share and discuss.

Cynthia and Patrick are still enthusiastic readers, even though they're too old for bedtime stories. Cynthia obtained a part-time job at a bookstore, allowing her to become acquainted with thousands of books. The only problem is where to find more bookshelves in their book-burdened home.

Show the Way.

28. Be humble; teach the wholeness of things

When children are to learn something new, wise parents have their children experience the new phenomenon in its wholeness. Looking at the picture on the cover of a jigsaw puzzle first helps someone put the pieces together, even though there are additional skills that come from studying the pieces. A person can best learn to ski down a hill if they first watch others ski down a hill. Breaking learning down into small parts can be useful, but knowing the pieces still leaves much to understand about the entire concept. Practice with dribbling, shooting, passing, and rebounding does not make a basketball player.

Help your child to hear the complete song before learning the notes.

Dot and John both loved being outdoors. They believed that the best times of all were those spent camping and hiking, and they wanted their children to enjoy being out in nature as much as they did. They decided that not only would a trip to the mountains teach their teens a great deal about nature, but it would provide lessons in persistence and resourcefulness.

They made a plan: Mom and Dad were going off on an adventure with five kids, all with backpacks and hiking shoes. They would take a full-blown camping and hiking trip. The entire family got together to discuss the date and the kinds of things that each person would have to get ready. John and Dot chose Onion Valley as the destination because it was already a comfortable, natural retreat for them. They would all appreciate its relative closeness to home, its convenient campsites, its great scenic beauty, and its trails with gentle climbs. The family of seven required a great amount of paraphernalia in order to go camping, but each person was responsible for gathering his or her own gear and was also responsible for one aspect of the family's equipment. The preparations went well.

Onion Valley proved a perfect campsite, complete with two picnic tables, water, and plenty of trees to shade the tent camper. After settling in, the family enjoyed a simple supper, cooked partly on the camp stove and partly over the campfire. It was a home away from home. After everyone ate and the dishes were done, they enjoyed singing a set of songs around the campfire. Then everyone went to sleep with parental admonitions to get plenty of rest for the big day ahead. Early in the morning, they would leave their camp site.

All that was made clear about the hike was that this was *not* going to be sauntering to a picnic. There would be plenty of walking and climbing. Although they had been on the trails out of Onion Valley before, John and Dot didn't remember exactly what was coming. They didn't do a detailed study of topographical maps, but instead they decided just to follow the trail markers to see what would happen. Their curiosity was as genuine as the kids'. The main rule for the day: Don't destroy the land. Everyone was expected to stay on the marked trails. Flowers were to be enjoyed wherever they grew and left alone.

There was plenty of puffing and panting at the start, coupled with one set of fallen arches and several bouts of "you made me do this" grumbling. But along the way they stopped for several welcome breaks with snacks of trail mix and lots of water. The tall mountains and vast landscapes provided a beautiful setting. Later, everyone enjoyed a leisurely lunchtime over their backpack lunches, sitting on rocks, enjoying mountainside sights and sounds.

As the hours went by, everyone came to see that they could go beyond what they thought they could do, parents included. They all walked on through aspen, up small steep trails, near small streams, and past frozen patches of snow, even though it was summer, to enjoy great vistas.

Everyone had something to offer. Polly was the family member who was able to identify trees along the way and Ralph was able to label the strata of rocks. Irma knew many of the wildflowers and John was good at identifying the few birds that they saw. Irma could also be encouraging to everyone and Joe was the one who could make things seem funny along the way. Dot laughed a lot. No one person was in charge. Instead, the leadership changed as the trail and time of day varied. John was in charge of getting everyone to turn back in plenty of time to relax before dinner. As it turned out, John and Dot were the last ones to take off their dusty boots back at the campsite after a long day on the trail. The other five eager hikers beat them back.

That week, they all went on several more hikes. After their initiation, some questions came up that needed answering. Family members were able to learn the answers from another one. How do you keep the water from leaking out of a canteen? What sunscreen works better? What is moleskin? Why do you prefer two pairs of socks? What if you hate wearing hats? How many miles is it to the lake? The time was spent well, building pride in their outdoor skills and compiling sweet memories for everyone.

Whole ideas and gathering thoughts from others come before pieces of ideas and sending thoughts to others.

29. Follow the middle road; it is the heart of knowing

Balancing the elements of various philosophies or lifestyles is part of the way for wise parents. They know that if their parenting reflects only one style, they cannot meet the varying needs of their different children. Parents find little success in being authoritarian and experience just as little when they are extremely laissez faire. The middle road is like the intersection of varying sets; it is not a pathway with unique properties of its own, nor is it merely straddling a fence. Wise parents know that they must

*come to mutual understandings with each other first, avoiding
arguments that worry their children; then they can establish
boundaries, not barriers, and allow freedom, but not negligence.
The Tao of the middle road allows parenting to be versatile, yet
unified.*

*Look for ways in which you can center yourself where com-
mon features of diverse philosophies converge. Your own philosophy will be pivotal.*

Carl and Kate put it this way: "When it comes to rules, you can't
have many absolutes. There are always adjustments to be made
for each child and set of circumstances." They know that Holly
is rather precise and tends to be a rule-oriented individual herself.
On the other hand, Corey is laid back about most situations. His
easygoing nature means that he has also needed parental guidance at times.

The Flanagans acknowledge that they have made mistakes
along the way. There were times when they should have said no.
The forces of peer pressure are not just on young people, but can
affect parents as well. They think, "If *those* parents think this is
OK, who am I to say no?"

Corey attended parties every weekend during the fall of his
sophomore year. His parents knew that he was with the same
kids from his parochial high school. Carl and Kate were under
the impression that these were "good kids" and that the parties
would be supervised. One Sunday, however, when Kate was going through pockets as she did the laundry, she found several
beer tops, and realized that they'd been too naive about the party
situation. With beer tops in hand, she had a long conversation
with Corey, setting forth their family's no-nonsense philosophy
about alcohol and driving. Corey knew very clearly where both
his parents stood. At about the same time, Corey was in the
process of making new friends who were involved in various
sports and school activities. He ended up not hanging out with
the beer-drinking friends at all as he became closer to kids with
other standards and interests.

On the other hand, even when intuition told Kate and Carl that attending a post-prom party in a hotel room wasn't wise, they ended up allowing their sensible daughter to go. After all, her date *was* the student body president—a boy with respected parents, and a decent reputation himself. Besides, the hotel was very refined. Holly crooned a tune very familiar to most parents: "I'll be the only one who isn't going." So Kate and Carl gave their permission.

As things transpired, the liquor flowed, the lights were low, and the music was full of romance. After a horrible scene with her date, Holly ended up calling her girlfriend and asking her to bring her home. The details remain sketchy to this day; luckily, Holly was able to get out of the situation, but Carl and Kate never did feel right about permitting the hotel visit in the first place.

Not that saying no is always best. Far from it. Kate and Carl have watched the impact of a "mostly no" parent on Holly's friend, Fay. In the elementary grades, Fay's mother was insistent that her daughter could stay overnight at no one's house except Holly's; even then, she was expected to "check in" at home several times. Once she stayed overnight and the girls decided to go over to another friend's house in the morning for a while. Fay's mother not only got furious that she had not been contacted, but she called the other girl's parents and accused them of inviting Fay without her permission. She was so strict as to seem irrational to most people. As a result, Fay began to do everything behind her mother's back. She spent her high school years running around, sneaking out, and proving that she was good at covering her tracks.

Corey also had a friend, Brian, who was never allowed to stay anywhere overnight except at the Flanagans'. (For some reason, Carl and Kate seemed trustworthy as parents to other moms and dads.) Brian, however, always felt that he couldn't do anything, and Corey's comment, "He cannot breathe," seemed to be on target. Brian even ventured a question in his high school health class one day: "Is it considered child abuse if a parent never lets a child do anything?" Brian did everything his parents wanted, however. He managed to earn a fine scholar/athlete award and then a scholarship for the coming year ... to a university in a state two thousand miles away.

Do not strive for extremes. Find peace in your heart and enjoy being parents.

30. Avoid using force; don't push

Effective motivation of children is not an obvious practice. In the Tao, however, parents are clear that self-discipline does not flourish in an atmosphere where negative, harsh threats and punishments are used. The parent who yanks a whining son or daughter by the arm at the supermarket is unwise and could hurt the child. Parents who spank their child as a punishment for hurting someone else are making a mistake, modeling the very behavior they seek to stop. Severe spankings—or worse—are simply not acceptable.

Wise parents encourage their children to participate in positive activities. As often as possible, they allow children to follow their interests. Forcing children to do things that they don't want to do usually backfires, but an ongoing attitude of "try it, you might like it" can promote curiosity and growth.

Ask your children what they would like to do and guide them to ways of accomplishing those things. Expect them to give activities a chance, but don't demand that they stick with all ventures. Childhood is for exploration.

Lew and Margaret have been clear-sighted and in agreement about avoiding negatives and punishments as much as possible.

Consequences for misbehavior have included loss of television or computer privileges for several days or being grounded. The longest consequence that anyone can recall was seven days long. The ongoing duration of a consequence doesn't need to be gigantic. Margaret and Lew hear about month-long groundings and have been glad that that has never seemed warranted at their house. They wonder who's being punished by some things.

The Williams children have had a variety of opportunities to develop different talents and interests. Their family has belonged to a local church for years, following a longstanding tradition in both Margaret's and Lew's families. As participants in the church youth program, Cynthia and Patrick helped put on musicals two, sometimes three, times a year. After various shows, many people have come up to Cynthia or to Patrick and exclaimed about their performance and talent. Because there are many other opportunities in their town for youth to join school and community musicals, Lew and Margaret have suggested each year that their kids try out for one of those. Each year, despite parental comments like, "But you'd be so good," the answer has been, "No, thanks. It isn't fun. Too much work. Boring rehearsals." And the parents have not pushed any harder.

When Cynthia was in fourth grade, she went out for a community basketball program with her friend Anne. They ended up on different teams, however. Cynthia's team was mostly boys, except for one other girl who had grown up as the little sister in a family of boys who treated her like one of them. Playing the games was difficult and nervewracking for Cynthia; she would hang back and avoid handling the ball in games, despite the fact that she was assertive in many other situations. Still, she never complained.

Lew and Margaret were sitting in the stands with their friend Bill, Anne's dad, one Saturday afternoon. He had a strategy: for every aggressive move on Cynthia's part, a fifty-cent award would be tallied up. The parents all thought they had a great incentive plan, and when they presented it later, Cynthia seemed to like the idea, too. But this bribe system made little difference in the long run. As a matter of fact, Cynthia later explained that it made her even *more* nervous. She dropped out of basketball until she played again in high school for two years. Then that was that, except for "goofing around" when a ball and a court were available.

Lew and Margaret have also realized that *making* a child choose a career path or go to a specific college can build resistance in their children. Demanding that kids take lessons because they have talent at certain things doesn't work. Insisting that the teenagers attend all events with the family benefits no one.

That doesn't mean that invitations and encouragement stop. It just means that expectations should not be rigid.

Contests of will benefit no one. Do not try to overcome others; win only when you have no other choice.

31. There is no glory in victory

Parents who win an argument with their children do not really win their children over. A winner on one side always means there's a loser on the other. It signifies lack of harmony or understanding. There is nothing of which to be proud when there is a loss of humanity or humility. Full empowerment happens only in win-win situations. A family with a win-lose environment is full of tension, manipulation, and oneupmanship.

If you have won a battle with your children, you have diminished their pride in thinking for themselves. Find a way for both of you to win. Only peace can bring wholeness.

Although Mapita's boys are considered "model" children by most of the outside world, the work of being their parent is seldom easy. Differences in perspectives arise over and over again between a woman with strong cultural ties to slower paced, traditional ways of living and sons who are growing up in the fast-paced urban context of turn-of-the-millennium Southern California.

Samuel refers to their Sunday meeting times as sort of like

NATO. He says that there are consequences for doing things that are wrong, but that the boys take their medicine, definitely without yelling, and usually without getting upset. Their mom talks, and they talk, and most things get pretty much talked out.

One of the topics that seems to come up over and over is the role of sports in their lives. At one side of the spectrum of passion is Jacob, who could eat, sleep, and breathe wrestling, along with Samuel, who also loves wrestling. At the other end is Mapita, who thinks a stroll in the park is lovely. She sees life as an opportunity to develop wisdom, help others, and develop relationships. It worries her that the emphasis on sports in the school environment, and in society in general, is so lopsided. There is more room for goodness in daily life, and perhaps so much striving for glory is simply not necessary. Constant competition and the rigid discipline it requires merely intrudes on what, to her, is real life.

Mapita has encouraged Samuel and Jacob to see that competition out in their world of school can only bring problems. But, the twins do compete with each other frequently. One year, they competed over who made a nicer Mother's Day card for Mapita. She reminded them that within their cultural heritage, cooperation is highly valued. She told the boys that it would mean the most to her if they made one card together and got along while they made it. That has worked well over quite a few years, and she treasures the results.

Even though Samuel and Jacob are competitive, things do not get out of hand at the Sanchez house. The boys have never hurt each other physically, and their Sunday meetings are always very helpful. Many solutions are hammered out. "Okay, you get to ride in the front seat, but the back seat person gets to choose the radio stations. All right, I'll do the patio next week. We each have to iron our own shirts. We will both have dinner with the aunts."

Everything seems to even out. One year Jacob was receiving one honor after the other at school. He was named the highest officer in two organizations, and many smaller things seemed to just fall into his lap. The next year, however, the opposite occurred, and Samuel was the one to accept many honors and surprises.

In wrestling, the boys participate at different weights, and Mapita's advice, "If you compete, you'll both lose," has probably carried through at several points. The wasted energy of competition would sap their accomplishments. The "picking" at each other would diminish their relationship.

Weapons are not instruments that make people noble. In the Tao, slaughter is mourned, not celebrated. Peace has the highest value.

32. The Way cannot be mastered

Wise mothers and fathers know that there will always be an ebb and flow of learning to parent. Advice and guidebooks may light the flame, but the deepening of understanding must happen within the individual. Parents make mistakes, but they can learn from them by resolving them for themselves. To equate a mistake with being "wrong" damages the integrity of the individual.

Learn from your mistakes. The Tao is a process, not a destination.

Joe, Dot's son from her previous marriage, had been raised with proper Southern manners. Not only was he very polite, but also he was a bright, mathematically inclined young man. He was well liked at school, and he became the president of the eighth-grade class. But as the new brother in the family he was not well liked at first—not at all.

In fact, Joe was treated poorly. Not only did his stepbrother and stepsisters give him problems, but the whole neighborhood of kids went against him in many ways. He was locked in the cupboard. He was picked on. The other kids taught him how to curse, and then proceeded to point out his bad words. They buried him up to his head at the beach. On it went, and as hard as Dot worked to prevent these problems, she couldn't eliminate them altogether.

Initially, she tried scolding and lecturing. Then she appealed to John to support her words. Soon she realized that they couldn't say enough and they couldn't get it right. Punishments given to the others seemed to make things get even harder for Joe. But they made sure that Joe knew they cared for him, and they told him that they supported his decisions about how to handle the bullying. They were clear about their love for each other and for their children. Lots of it.

As time went on, some things got better. There were more and more positive interactions, and ultimately, Joe was right there with the rest of the kids when they had their jump-on-the-bed contests . . . or when they were caught leaping off the roof when their parents were gone.

Do not attempt to add legs to a snake.

33. Know yourself; the influence of virtue is immortal

To develop inner knowledge is to gain insight. In the Way, parents go beneath the surface and make decisions based on their reflections and their self-knowledge. Mothers and fathers are complex people with many talents and skills. Those who are successful in their work arenas may overlook how their creative or organizational abilities can help them to relate at home. They often sell themselves short.

Parents who realize which of their efforts have made an impact and which haven't have at least stepped on the pathway to future success. When a parent concludes that a string of ever-increasing consequences for a child's misbehavior has not changed the behavior, it is time to look at what changes the parent can make . . .

in herself or himself, not the child. The parent who can look within to know will recall what has been tried and what has been effective.

Reflect on the values that you believe in and recognize that when you have taken care of yourself, you will be better able to take care of others. Take a look at what you have done well and what you would like to do better. This caring to know will have positive effects for you and your children, for you will not give up.

Dot is a gardener. To her, gardening is a metaphor for her ways of dealing with life. Although she loves to interact with people, and she does that well, she needs to spend time alone in her garden to think and gather strength.

Even as a child, she spent a great deal of time outdoors, playing and walking in the family garden and orchard. When she did good things, she was given a flower garden of her own as a reward. She was always there, in the garden, preparing the soil, making neat rows, nurturing seedlings, and enjoying the results of her labor.

Dot believes she is who she is because she grew up in a family atmosphere of open hospitality and generosity. She shared her belongings with friends. Even giving a new dress to a needy friend was acceptable: No matter how "bad" a person's reputation, they were welcome in the family home. Nurturing others was this family's way.

In contrast to Dot's childhood patches, her gardens as a grownup are never in neat rows. She has become a plot planter, throwing a few seeds here and more over there. She raises organic vegetables and tosses the flowers in the same vicinity as the leafy greens. Then she mixes them all with other kinds of things "in order to confuse the pests." Dot and John have moved frequently over the years, from one home to another and from one state to another. Many aspects of their lives have been full of turmoil. However, as with her gardens, she always wants life's boundaries to be clear. But it's okay for the internal conditions to be somewhat chaotic and full of freedom.

As an adult, Dot still goes out of her way to help friends, even if it makes things seem confusing and disorderly. Would you like to sleep on the couch? Go ahead! Do you need us to drive up to Chicago from Arkansas to do that? Okay. Sounds like fun. Sure, we'll just put that in our trailer and take it for you.

To know others is to be wise. To know oneself is to be enlightened.

34. Do not strive for greatness

When the wise parent is least insistent, greatness will come. Great parenting isn't found in grand lectures and impressive rulebooks. Simple opportunities for children to spend time with their parents in a variety of situations can be highly instructive. Success in parenting usually means that children will thrive under subtle, but high, expectations.

How you appreciate the world around you and respect your children can be shown in a variety of ways. Be yourself in your enjoyment of life.

As Margaret explains, a lot of teenagers want their parents to disappear for a good part of the day. They say and do things that are mortifying. It's OK to be there to prepare supper—if it's something good that night. It's OK to be there if you are willing to drive them somewhere they want to go. It's certainly good to be there if they need help with a sticky homework problem. Otherwise, it would be fine to depart for another planet.

Cynthia suggested that maybe Margaret shouldn't come to her next cross-country meet. She said that Margaret had stuck out like a sore thumb since she was the *only* parent there that day, and she had actually had the "nerve" to yell words of encouragement to Cynthia and her teammates as they ran by. When Margaret explained that she was planning to be at the next meet but she was going with the mother of one of the other runners, it was better—not OK, but better, because if you are going to be embarrassed, at least someone else is there to be embarrassed with you.

At the next meet Margaret sat in the bleachers next to the mom and dad of a boy from the opposing team. They explained that they went to all of the meets. They were, however, not allowed to say *anything* when their son went by. He had made it clear that he didn't want any yelling or encouragement. Even his little sister watches him run by with her mouth sealed shut. What they do, instead, is yell for his teammates; but when *he* runs by, they clam up. This is all right with him.

Margaret concluded that she would honor some requests, but some things were just going to continue whether Cynthia was embarrassed or not. The rules were that no personal secrets or criticisms would ever be aired; no naked baby pictures would be shown, and no embarrassing moment stories would be told. That meant that Margaret continued exclaiming about the wonderful shapes of the clouds, Lew continued his singing in the car, and Margaret went on holding conversations with Cynthia's friends, asking about family, school, and homework. Margaret also kept up her habit of chatting with strangers in line or with the clerks at the supermarket, the post office, or the department store. These embarrassing moments were how Lew and Margaret felt that they were modeling the ways that they navigated daily life. They didn't pretend to be anything but themselves.

Do not make claims for yourself; greatness will come to you.

35. The Way has its own rhythm; use it

In the Tao, life can be plain, peaceful, and restful amid turmoil and change. People who engage in activities that are intrinsically highly motivating end up losing track of time. They can go for hours without getting tired. The Tao permits a tireless state. So it can be with parenting. Parents can learn how their family best falls into a state of timelessness. It may be that some contexts are better than others to meet the whole family's needs.

You will find that some ways of life will benefit you all. Recognize and appreciate what those are, for even though they may be temporary or even occasional, they will set the tone and establish memories for days and years to come. Follow the pattern, get the beat, and let the beat go on. You will want to get lost in your work.

The Williams family frequently vacations at Indian Lake in Michigan. There, on Wa-ma-el-na Island, the family lives in a log cabin that was once part of an old fish camp. Grandmother Williams is usually there in another small cabin, and Lew's Aunt Martha and Uncle George are always there, because it is their little island. Other members of their extended family are usually there, too. There are more tricks and teasing if Uncle Dan comes, more fishing if Uncle Robert's around.

The rhythm of each day is determined by the positions of the sun. Clock time seems unimportant, and schedules seem artificial. The only things the family has to do are prepare meals, clear the brush around the house, and make sure whatever appliances they need are in good working order. There are plenty of choices to make and challenges to meet, but they are mostly pleasurable. Grandmother's "cukes" are delicious. The loon warbles across the lake, the clouds move across the sky, and the wind blows through the birch leaves. Fish dart about in clear water. Everyone knows that it feels good just to sit on the warm smooth boards of the long dock and watch a red and white bobber on the shining water.

Margaret likes to read while lounging in a cushioned chair on the porch with a gentle breeze puffing on her cheek now and then. Cynthia loves to swim and snorkel, splashing off to Ice House Island and back, then resting in a soft, giant inner tube, warmed by the sun as little waves lap against the rocky shore.

Patrick thinks it's fine to sit on the lodge porch where tiny shadows dapple his sketch pad as he draws and draws. And Lew is in heaven standing hip deep in cool water several feet off the north shore. He casts and waits, watching golden ripples on the water, perhaps to catch a fish.

Margaret likes a quote from Art Buchwald that she cut out of the newspaper: "The best things in life aren't things."

Swim with the current; its uses are limitless.

36. The weak and the tender overcome the hard and the strong

Wise parents know that yielding can slowly prevail. Just as someone who fishes knows that "the large and powerful fish should not be taken from deep waters," parents know that a child is not going to respond well to parental force. They do not attempt the impossible but recognize that a child's stubborn strength can become thoughtful agreement in response to patient parental caution, reservation, flexibility, sincerity, and honesty. In the Tao, a parent must be willing to meet a strong or difficult adversary on his or her own ground.

Admit your own mistakes, and allow your sons and daughters to "set the hook" through their own aggression. Reel in slowly, carefully, steadily. Do not bellow and bluster, for you will blunder. Offer gently those guiding comments that will help your children to think things through "on their own." Catch them being good.

Few day-to-day disappointments have turned into major problems at the Flanagans. There is usually plenty of opportunity for conversation at meals and on the weekends, so most things get worked out little by little. It was, therefore, quite a surprise for Carl and Kate to realize that a situation was getting out of hand with Corey. He was acting cocky, and it wasn't just now and then. The idea of being an upperclassperson at school had gone to his head. He was treating freshmen as badly as he had been treated, perhaps worse. "*You* don't even *think* of walking ahead of me, you lowly freshman. Hey, freshman, you want to take a look at some trash?" He was acting like a real meathead, and, after it had been going on for a while, he came home and started to brag about it.

Kate knows she didn't do well at first. Her first response was to lecture. "I can't believe this. You are doing the very thing you hated *other* people doing to you! You're acting like a jerk."

Corey responded, "No matter what I say, you are always judging me. I'm never going to tell you *anything*!"

Kate's knee-jerk responses were a failure. She knew she hadn't said things at the right time, and she knew she hadn't said things in the right way. She had made a mistake for sure, so she didn't say anything more in a critical way that day at all.

Instead, she decided to point out to Corey the ways in which he was caring with other kids, especially those younger than he. Corey was always good to his cousins, most of whom were younger than he. Kate remembered to tell him how nice it was of him to spend time with them and make them feel special. Corey was a host for the Special Olympics track meet that was held on his campus, and Carl and Kate also made a point of remembering to tell him how really special *he* had been. "They really liked being with you. Did you see how happy they were when you helped them? You've learned a lot of lessons for when you become a father. It's always important to listen to young children. They won't forget you."

His parents also recognized that sharing good reflections with Corey wasn't something that could just come up in general conversation. "Hi. Welcome home from school. Have a snack and, by the way, you sure were good at the Olympics." No, that wouldn't work. Talking about tender things tended to need tender moments—relaxed time when listening really could take place. Maybe a comment during a back scratch for their son. Maybe another comment with a Coke float at the end of the evening. Comments need to be made at the right time, not just in the right way. As parents, the Flanagans have tried to develop intuition about both.

When Corey was a senior, he was honored at several events during the course of the year, and he was given compliments in many ways. But one of the most special kudos that settled very warmly on Kate's and Carl's ears was given by a young member of the football team at an end-of-year awards banquet dinner Corey's junior year. "Corey was always the one who looked out for the newcomers on the team. He was there to help us, and he always treated us right."

Little can match the power of water, though it may be soft and supple.

37. Seek simplicity and honor what is known

Parents in the Tao realize that their children know a great deal about things that their parents never learned in school. Many of the things that students of the 1960s studied in the sciences at high school and college are part of the eighth grade—perhaps even sixth grade—curriculum near the turn of the century. Classes on current events, drug awareness courses, and cross-cultural assemblies are just a few of the opportunities that children have . . . and parents don't. Mothers and fathers are often perplexed by their offspring's "deafness" to questions such as: "What did you learn at school today?" Sometimes parents can ask questions or raise issues that come out of reading the newspapers and that relate to subjects their children are studying in school. Otherwise, parents must take alternate routes into the complex worlds and knowledge bases of their own children.

Your children know many things. Respect their knowledge and find ways to understand it.

Carl and Kate are like many parents; their first child has influenced them to change their behaviors with child number two.

While Holly was in junior high, and then in her early years of high school, her parents weren't expecting specific things from her as far as schooling went. Both parents had been to college, but neither had been a particularly diligent student. Their prevailing attitude about their daughter's school progress was to go along with the flow—"You want to do it? That's fine." One day, when Holly was a junior, her counselor told her that, if she kept up with the pace she had set in her studies and activities, she would probably be the class valedictorian. This unusual occasion prompted everyone to think about the implications of education in new ways, and Holly, especially, began to encourage her mom and dad that there were some things that they should expect of her as parents.

Kate and Carl realized that Holly had done many things as a result of her personality and interests, and those things contributed to her success in school. Holly showed them that she had come up with internal pep talks, partly from her parents' influences and the times spent with other members of their extended family, and partly from her own thinking: School is a responsibility. You can be whatever you want to be. Don't be shy. Hold your self-expectations high. Stick with things. Be a team player. Try to see things in a positive light. Be a friend.

So, as good things continued to transpire for Holly, her mom and dad proceeded to learn what values seemed to be of real importance in pursuing an education and succeeding. Holly is quite certain that what she taught her mom and dad were ideas that they could stress as parents for their second child.

Learn from the children. You don't need to know it all.

38. Virtue is its own reward; differences arise when the Way is lost

In the minds of the best parents, parenting is in and of itself a re-
ward. Wise parents expect to do well. A parent wears many hats,
including that of lifelong learner. Good parents do not expect to
be given status or wealth, and they are examples of intrinsic mo-
tivation at its best, for when something must be done, they do it
without special reward. Problems are always going to occur
along the way, but in the Tao, parents anticipate tomorrow with
optimism and a sense that in the long run, the work will be
worth the effort.

Do not expect compensation for the many facets of the work
you must accomplish as a parent. Once you accept a position,
with its related "pay scale," you do what you must to get the job
done well. If you help young people to create and fulfill their
dreams, that is enough.

John knows that having children can present problems, even in
the best of times. Children are children; they don't always coop-
erate, they sometimes get in trouble, and accidents do happen.
When Dot and her kids moved in with John and his kids, Ralph's
drums took up most of the dining room. Since family meals were
being instituted at the time, the dining room was needed, and
Ralph's drums needed a new home. John helped his stepson set
his drum kit up in a shed off the patio by the dining room, and
some ground rules were established. Drum practice could be
from 2:00 to 3:30 P.M. every day. Everything was set, and all
seemed well.

What no one but Ralph knew for a long time, however, was
that a woman who lived up the hill always took an afternoon
nap at the same time as his designated practicing. This particular
neighbor was very disturbed by the drumming and called the police,

not once but several times. During one of a string of police visits, Dot arrived home early from work and learned about the neighborhood predicament. Ralph had never told his parents about the problem and had managed to negotiate the situation on his own to that point. He always assured the officers that he would keep it down. Furthermore, the police had never contacted them, much to their surprise. It took negotiations among the neighborhood grown-ups to settle the question about appropriate playing times and get things smoothed over in the neighborhood, but the case of the afternoon drummer did finally get resolved. John and his stepson Joe worked hard on a large-scale garage soundproofing project. Spaces around the doors were stuffed, walls were covered, old carpeting was laid, and Ralph resumed practice on his drums.

John also remembers a time when the job of caring for the church lawn fell to him each Saturday. He decided to pay Ralph and Joe several dollars for their assistance. Before any mowing could be done, several other tasks were necessary: edging the lawn, sweeping the walks, trimming the bushes and trees, and picking up papers. The boys simply had no interest at all in picking up papers—until John made paper pickup a requirement before either young man would be allowed to get up on the small tractor mower.

Over several weeks, Ralph tried to pull seniority on his stepbrother to get more driving time on the mower, but for a while at least, the rule was that each boy had so many minutes per turn. Then the whole project paled for Ralph. In spite of the monetary benefits, he did not, could not, care about the lawn job. He ended up staying home and finding other things to do that were important to him, and he was ultimately granted permission to do other tasks, as long as he was being helpful to others in some way. In the meantime, Joe was grateful to be the only son on the church lawn project because he got to be the mower operator-rider all the time. John picked up the papers.

At about the same time, when Natalie was not quite eight, she was hit by a car while riding her blue bike to the library. She was knocked over as she crossed the street at a corner, and her arms and legs and face were seriously scraped and bruised. Luckily she did not require emergency treatment, and the paramedics who arrived on the scene were able to understand her as she recited her phone number. They called, finding John home from work on one of those rare occasions when he'd come home from a business meeting in another city. He took Natalie home, and all was well.

Natalie was fine, but Dot was not. It wasn't that she hadn't cared for her child, but she felt that she should have been there, instead of at the university in a class she was taking. After that, Dot decided that she would only leave for class after everyone was safely tucked away in their after-school activities; no latch-key kids for her. What happened was that she got a C in the class, changing the pattern of top grades that she'd previously received in her program. Still, for her it was worth knowing that the children had been transported to safe places and were where they needed to be. Dot recognized that her lateness made her a thorn in her instructor's side, but the kids had to come first. Dot was the first to applaud when she discovered that the next classes she needed were moved to a later time slot. Her peace of mind was restored, and so was her grade point average.

Hold the Way with conscience; do not expect a reward.

39. Humility brings honor

Parents are each unique individuals. Having grown up in different contexts, they will not always think in identical ways, despite their efforts to present a united front. Nevertheless, they need to avoid promoting their own ideas or negating their spouse's through comments or actions that imply or declare, "I am right and s/he is wrong." When perspectives are different, one is not intrinsically better. It takes calm deliberation and, usually, quite a

*long time to establish which idea is more appropriate to a situa-
tion. Children should be included in the decision making.*

   *Get beyond your ego. Be sincere, when you say, "In my hum-
ble opinion."*

Mapita met her husband when she traveled in Italy. He seemed to
fit her image, based on her sister's Italian husband, of Italian men
as warm, responsible, and gentlemanly. Unfortunately, Mapita's
stereotype was shattered early in the relationship, for the real individual was austere and disinterested in exploring life's exciting
offerings. He saw his role as a future father as being that of the
provider, taking care of food, clothing, a house, and bills. Beyond
being someone who would take care of those basic needs, he
thought, would be frivolous and not within his "job descrip-
tion." Mapita realized that as husband and wife they were constantly clashing over very basic values and assumptions about
marriage. She believed that husbands helped make houses into
homes. She needed someone who cared as much as she in setting
up a warm family relationship, providing for moral education
and future attitudes. Their divorce was inevitable. Nevertheless,
she believed that the decisions about their relationship should
not keep the children from knowing and respecting their father.

   Mapita never downplays the importance of her former husband to her sons. Certainly, many physical and temperamental
traits have come to the boys from their dad. As years have gone
by, her former husband has never come to the United States. Still,
the boys have gotten to know their papa because of their own visits to Europe. For those opportunities the boys—and Mapita—
are grateful.

   The boys have been to Italy because it is the homeland of their
father, and they have met relatives on his side of the family several times. One extended visit to an aunt and uncle's house in
Italy in a small city right between Rome and Venice, gave the
boys a chance to know the pleasures of Italian culture. They
asked permission to work at the family business, a small pizza
restaurant with a walk-up window. They had daily interactions

with members of the community and helped to make the dough for pizza. Customers could order spaghetti, drinks, or pizza and either sit at small tables or take the food away.

As the boys enter adulthood, they both dream of returning to Italy and traveling to many small villages. Their father does not live in Italy now, however. He has been a guest worker in Germany for many years, employed by a firm that makes precision medical equipment.

Because of their ties to Italy, both boys see Italian food as being the most delicious cuisine in the world, and their ideas of a great night out include enjoying a meal at a fancy Italian restaurant. They consider their Italian heritage to be equal in importance to their Mexican-American lineage.

To achieve oneness is to be fulfilled. The greatest sculptures seem to emerge from the clay. The wise parent will not boast.

40. Something comes from nothing; nothing comes from something

Wise parents recognize that the interactions of polarities help promote understanding. Tension does accompany learning, and children must have opportunities to disagree and find resolutions to their differences. You can't have life without death. You need both the male and the female ways. You need the high with the low. The Way promotes oneness.

Permit your children to see opposing viewpoints on issues. You do not need to tell them which one to hold. In understanding one, they can better understand the other.

One Saturday morning when Holly was in the eighth grade, Kate dropped her off to attend an event at Our Lady of Hope, her school, for the morning. As Kate was driving home an hour later after doing some shopping, she saw a parade with people of all ages marching down Main Street . . . including her own daughter. There was Holly carrying a large, painted cardboard sign that read, "Don't kill an unborn child"! Kate was shocked. She hadn't known about the parade, and she felt even more baffled because the issue of reproductive choice had never been discussed at home.

When Carl and Kate picked Holly up at the school later, they expressed their surprise gently as they drove along. "Hi. Were we ever surprised to see you in the parade. We didn't know that you were marching today. What do they tell you at school about abortion? It is a very controversial thing."

"It's wrong. You can't kill an unborn child. It is a human being."

"That is certainly true. I don't think we could *ever* consider it. We do want you to know why some pretty decent people feel differently about abortion, though." Kate and Carl told Holly some of the reasons that abortion was legalized. In their teen years they had both known girls who had suffered through illegal abortions. One fifteen-year-old had been traumatized for life by a botched attempt at a home abortion with a coat hanger. The other had suffered physical problems after an illegal abortion across the border in Mexico and then had a difficult life, becoming a drug user and enduring bad relationships. They also told Holly about the terrible lives that some babies endure when they are born to parents who can't be responsible. In addition, they told her why they respected people who were part of the anti-abortion movement.

Carl and Kate also shared with their daughter that they definitely did not believe in abortion for themselves, but that they did understand why some people choose it. In this, and in other conversations that came along about controversial issues relating to matters like divorce and the death penalty, and prisons, the Flanagans wanted their daughter to know that there were opposing views, and that they all had a responsibility to know what all the facts and feelings were before making personal choices.

The right answer is that one answer may not be everyone's.

41. Appearances can deceive; the Way is known through intuition and tireless practice

Wise parents do not give up. They recognize that sometimes children may appear to be making little progress toward career choices or other major life decisions, but they do not lose sight of the Tao. Generations of children sometimes take years to become their "real" selves. It is good to encourage personal growth through activities that apply skills and knowledge. People who love music do music. People who love math do math. The evidence is there, but it is not always obvious, for people do math and music (and other things) in wide varieties of ways. Passionate listeners can become music critics, not musicians. People who enjoy long chains of logical thinking may become systems analysts, not mathematicians.

Do not be impatient with late bloomers. Look back to discover themes that have existed throughout your child's lifetime, whether it be art, relating to others, personal insights, speaking out, or other talents. Share your insights, but always know that your children must select the pathways of their own lives. Help them to unfold.

At school Ralph was the sort of student who did enough to get along, but he never enjoyed writing papers and taking tests. He was a dreamer, a drawer, and a drummer. When Dot met him— her new stepson—for the first time, she saw a handsome young man with a sweet face, light blond hair to his shoulders, a white bandanna circling his head. In her mind she wondered how it was that such a traditional man as John would have such an off-beat son. The father was a doer, but the child was a daydreamer who was classified as a "Title 1" student at his school because of his low test scores. He spent a great deal of time drawing pictures and not enough time doing homework.

Dot was sure that she would get used to the unusual ways of this young man, and she was sure that he would get used to her, despite the fact that he missed the first few hours of her wedding on purpose. But she wasn't really ready for his bedroom. On the white paint of its four walls were ink drawings and writings, sketches, cartoons, caricatures, poetry, quotations, and exclamations. Her reaction to the wild bedroom, as she was getting settled in the new home, John's place, made her realize she'd have a lot of work to do on her own thinking, for she felt very prudish, terribly straight, and quite formal.

Ralph was interested in art and drumming. He was involved with the school yearbook and was designated as the cover artist one year, and his drum set was a full kit with plenty of potential sounds.

Ralph's extreme independence was coupled with the fact that, as Dot puts it, this offbeat boy was one of the sweetest, kindest, gentlest people in the world. Like all the Singleton kids, he went to church—mostly whichever one happened to be where the fun was at the time. He washed pans at a daycare center.

Ultimately, he became very interested in a particular church. Homework and cracking the books had never been his way, but with new motivations, he ultimately finished college as a religion major.

He was then sponsored to do religious work in Japan, where he came to be in great demand as a spiritual leader. His fine ear allowed him to become fluent in Japanese. His personality endeared him to people in his new cultural environment, and he came to work with three different churches there, performing Western-style weddings, with white dresses and all the trimmings, as part of his regular duties. He also plays his drums in all three churches. His ability to move others is admired. He also has a special girlfriend and, John and Dot say, he will get married when he will. He's always worked through to his decisions in a rather slow, wandering, tentative way, but he's kept his commitments when he finally gets to making them.

Great characteristics are not always obvious.

42. Harmony is to be achieved through the blending of the passive and the active—the *yin* and the *yang*

A child's needs are best met when two types of dynamic parenting forces interact. It is not unusual for two parents to deal with a situation in different ways. Drawing out a child through insight and intuition (yin) always works in concert with times of assertive direction and explanation (yang). Two parents may fulfill two interacting roles, but one parent may very well provide both influences, or both parents may each represent a balanced mix as well. Traditionally, yin forces are thought of as feminine, and yang as masculine, but a mother's parenting might be very yang in contrast to a father's yin ways. If a child behaves inappropriately, the mother may be the one who resets the standards and clarifies the probable consequences, while the father might watch the situation play itself out through natural consequences. It is all right for two parents to have different styles, as long as they are compatible and do not send two conflicting messages to their children.

Do not hesitate to send direct messages as long as children are also allowed to construct their own meanings and values from the lessons so vividly taught by life.

After John and Dot's wedding, they moved into John's house with their children from their past marriages. It wasn't long before the results of their past discipline systems became clear. Dot's children were used to a regimen of daily chores and weekly schedules. She had expected the house to be clean at all times. John's kids, on the other hand, had been part of a very loose structure in their dad's first family home. Chores were incidental, children were free spirits, and adults were the chore organizers (and workers). His previous home was not unsanitary, but it was seldom tidy—except for his own bedroom, which was immaculate.

In their new family setting, John's children felt Dot was an extremely authoritarian mother. They resented being told to do this and do that. On the other hand, Dot's children quickly saw John as a laissez-faire dad who was easy to get along with but who let them get away with a lot of things.

One day when Dot arrived home after a trip to the supermarket, as she entered the house she heard loud squeals of delight mixed with yowls of complaints. There, in the dining room, was a slide playground. The children had pulled two mattresses off twin beds and propped them on and against the large, oval dining table. The setup allowed two riders to slide quickly to the floor at once, while the others climbed onto the table to prepare for their rides. With their odd number, there was a great deal of thumping and bumping and pushing and screaming. The five children were creating chaos.

Dot yelled, "Stop!" in a clear, firm voice. "This is unacceptable. Our dining room is not a playground. And mattresses aren't slides." Then she had the children clean up. "Set each mattress back neatly. Put the sheets on straight and tuck them in. Put the covers on with the round edge at the foot of the bed." Then she sent them outside.

Later, she and John discussed the incident and decided that some changes would have to be made. While John admired the children's ingenuity and revealed his feelings that kids will be kids, he recognized the potential for disaster. Dot was appalled at the mess and the possible dangers to the children and the furniture, but she had to smile at the group's togetherness. Their task, as they saw it, was to be consistent and make lemonade out of the event's lemons. The mattress incident wasn't the first chaotic event of this sort, and it wouldn't be the last, but they needed to reduce the probability that something like that would happen again. When the family was eating dinner together, John and Dot made several things clear. No more dismantling of furniture without permission. Safety is the most important thing to consider. Responsibility is to be shared in this family.

They also made several proposals that needed everyone's agreement. A job chart needed to be made, with some choices and some rotating responsibilities. The children and the adults would work on it together. Everyone would have to decide: Where is the indoor place to play in this house? How messy can it get, and when will it be cleaned? By whom? What else needs to be done? Who is in charge of what?

Harmony is a group project. One may lose from a profit or profit from a loss.

43. Use your resources

Wise parents know that they model behaviors and share ideas through family experiences. They also realize that children learn from one another. Certainly younger children learn from the older ones, but there are also many ways that learning can happen in the reverse. Many of life's lessons can be learned from a variety of people.

Provide situations in which you and your children may learn from each other, but also know that many real events in life provide rich learning experiences, despite being totally unexpected. You need not say a word.

Patrick has watched his big sister all his life, and he says that she has shown him a lot over the years. All through school, he's learned songs from her, whether they were Sunday School songs complete with motions or enthusiastic camping songs from her sixth-grade week at Outdoor Education. When he was three and four, she was avid about playing school, especially when she got to be the teacher. She quizzed him on the sounds of the magnetic letters on the refrigerator and asked him questions about stories that they both knew. "What did Mr. McGregor grow in his garden? What did Peter have to do when he stayed home?" Patrick joins his sister in being an avid music and movie fan. He also sees, as she has shown him, that some things are to be taken seriously in life and some aren't really such a big deal. High school is just a step toward life. Don't get caught up with the trivial aspects of life. Don't be rude. Don't be a jerk. Be a hard worker.

Patrick, on the other hand, has taught Cynthia about perseverance, about patience, and about humor through the years. He has been a companion for her at many times—he even served as her escort on the football field when she had a weekend as a homecoming princess one fall. Although he has done his share of bugging his big sister, and she has done her share of bulldozing her little brother, the two siblings genuinely appreciate each other and spend time together.

Margaret also recalls that Cynthia and she may have "taught" a few lessons the day Cynthia fell into the canyon. Cynthia was out exploring in the yard with her friend Susan, another fifth-grader. As Margaret was chatting with her sister on a long-distance phone call, Susan walked in through the kitchen doorway, alone.

"Cynthia fell into the canyon!"

"Very funny, Susan. Is this another one of your jokes?"

"*Honest,* I'm telling the truth. This is no joke. She slid down the hill and she kept sliding on the grass and she can't climb out."

Then it hit.

"Oh, my God! Is she all right? Can she talk?"

"Yes."

"You go back to be with her. Talk to her! I'll be right there."

Susan had spoken so calmly that it all seemed like a bad joke—the kind that Cynthia loved to play, the Big Scare. But this was real. Margaret began to talk to herself with textbook care. Remain calm. Don't panic. She'll be all right. We'll get her out. There's nothing dangerous down in the arroyo. Or is there?

She tied on tennis shoes and ran out to their east yard, which descended to a tall row of eucalyptus trees that edged a steep, weedy canyon—a narrow crevice so deep that nobody had ever seen the bottom from any vantage point above.

Margaret slowly sidestepped down the slope, sliding with each step despite her caution, to the edge of the canyon.

"Are you all right? Cynthia, are you OK? Can you talk?"

"Yes. I'm stuck on this tree. I can't get out. I'm OK . . . but I'm real sore."

"Don't worry, honey. You'll be all right! Susan, you keep on talking to her. I'll be right back. I've got to get a rescue rope."

As it turned out, as Margaret was practicing her tosses to get the end of a rope down to Cynthia, her neighbor, Harry, walked by on the street above. He'd had forty years of experience walking on the steep hillside with surefooted steps in his work boots, and he was able to climb down and do all the right things to dislodge Cynthia.

Cynthia was sore, scraped, and bruised, and she took it easy for the rest of the day . . . and the next.

Patrick and Lew were surprised at the scene when they arrived home, and even more surprised to hear the story. They commented on how good it was that everyone was resourceful, remained calm, and listened to one another. Another parenting adventure was over, and everyone had learned something—including Patrick, who ventures near the canyon, but by other pathways.

Only masters can attain wordless teaching.

44. Know when to stop; preserve your health. Keep a sense of balance

Parents know that the multiple tasks of running a household and raising a family can be endless. In a world where so many mothers and fathers are working parents, the pressures are intensified. Still, in the Tao, they find ways to set priorities and limit their activities. Knowing that they can accomplish tasks better in the mornings or in the evenings, wise parents set aside those hours to plan and gather resources. Often the best plans include careful delegation of responsibilities. Children are capable and energetic. Friends, neighbors, and relatives can help carry out plans.

Decide on your personal limits and write down the things that you must, and want to do. Find ways to combine family business with family pleasure. Remember to reward yourself with things you want to do when you have accomplished the things you must do. Seek contentment.

Mapita always knew that she wanted her sons to have direct knowledge of their heritage and of Mexico, but she also knew that she couldn't provide that knowledge all by herself. In order to help the twins to keep up their language and culture and do something special for her profession as well, Mapita organized and supervised a summer language program for teachers in her own school district and nearby districts in her county. She took the boys and twelve teachers and traveled to Oaxaca for six summers in a row, performing a service for her colleagues that allowed them to deal effectively with the ever-growing number of Hispanic families in their own city in the United States.

Living in a hotel in Mexico was fun for two young American boys. They learned how to play chess and checkers with the elderly men who liked to spend their late afternoons in the lobby. They were allowed to explore the hotel as long as they weren't noisy and didn't disturb anyone. Spending time with a baby-sitter while their mom taught lessons during the day gave them an opportunity to play with Mexican children and practice their Spanish as well as learn new games. Part of the time, they went to a nursery school where they interacted with Mexican teachers and attended cultural events and field trips.

Because the boys were very well mannered, they were welcome to go many places, including cultural events that only much older kids would typically attend. Only events that would be totally inappropriate for kids their age would get crossed off the list. They got to visit a restaurant that featured pre-Columbian dances and, in spite of the loud drums, they fell asleep and slept through the whole show. They went to the Palace of Fine Arts in Mexico City and attended an evening Flamenco concert, keeping alert. The tempo of life in Oaxaca allowed the children to be responsible for themselves in many ways.

One year, Mapita decided to let the boys stay in Oaxaca and go to school there for six weeks while she returned to her work duties in the United States. Their baby-sitter was her dear friend, and she had often asked Mapita to allow the boys to stay and participate in school life in their "other" hometown. She was grateful for time alone to focus on her profession and still know that the boys were having a good experience. The boys were eleven years old and in the sixth grade. Mapita received several letters from them during their stay. They were usually typed with care on a typewriter. Here are two:

Dear Mom,
How are you doing? I am doing fine. Carlos and Juanita had a nice party for us. The pinata looked like Bart Simpson.

Over here we like school. We march a lot. We salute the flag outside. Every Monday we wear our gala uniform and it is all white with a red sweater. Today we read a poem in school. I knew it.

Dona Lupe is teaching us how to play jacks. Oh, mom. Candy the parrot does flips in her cage.

Love,
Samuel

P.S. I am having fun.
P.P.S. I love you.
P.P.P.S. Write back!

Another letter was half in Spanish, where Samuel was trying out his new written language abilities.

> Hola,
> Como estas estoy bien y apsendiando hablar a escribir en espaniol a mis amigos. La maestra es muy buena. En todo ella no is enojona. No pega los mionos.
>   I wrote in Spanish. Now sometimes it gets boring at school because girls ask me to be their boyfriend. I am mean. I said no. I get shivers. They can really bug you at recess.

When Jacob wrote he took a different approach.

> Dear Mom,
> I am listening to New Kids on the Block. Today is the new day. I am missing you a lot. One less week before we see you. This should come with a gift. I love you.
>
>   Jacob
> P.S. Correct my note. Copy, and send a copy back. And thank you.

The boys' experiences in their "other" culture affected their life at home. They had a new command of Spanish that helped them to communicate with community members and several relatives and helped them in their language studies at school. They came to understand the origins of certain events and sayings relating to Hispanic culture in their Southern California surroundings. Most of all, they got a newfound respect for their Mexican roots and Mapita had organized her school program and found time to relax a bit.

Those who know contentment don't exhaust their spirit.

45. Tranquillity is more important than perfection

An agitated, irritated parent cannot be effective. Wise parents find ways to become examples of tranquillity, incorporating quiet moments of reflection or meditation into the day. If they have to, they make the time and recognize that something else may not come out perfect. Parents have to be conscious of helping one another. Some can trade off middle-of-the-night feedings when their children are babies. As the children grow, the duties of attending sports events and parent meetings can be divided or done together, depending on what might bring pleasure to everyone, parents certainly included. When children become teens, the questions become: "Who does the late night pickups? Who waits up?"

Times of tranquillity evolve in different ways for different people. One person's perfection is another person's "hanging loose." Something that seems "up tight" in another's behavior may just be his or her way of staying centered. Many conflicts between individual parents and between parents and their children can be avoided if they all become aware of their differences.

Your pushing may promote excellence, but the child must have complete knowledge of the implications. The Olympic swimmer or gymnast in our society does not have a normal childhood.

Margaret recalls that when Cynthia, her first child, arrived, she felt the birth announcements had to be just so. They were to be hand-printed lithographs, with both the cover picture and interior message created through block printing technique. Thus, as a new mother, she sat at the kitchen table printing the announcements hour after hour, day after day, surrounded by linoleum blocks, brayers, inks, and special papers. Although she enjoyed the results, she got more and more tired. Getting up with Cynthia to nurse became more and more difficult, and although Lew was always willing to help, she soon found herself suffering from a case of postpartum blues.

When Patrick came along five years later, she decided that sending photocopied birth announcements would be just fine. In general, staying home with the second baby was certainly less tiring and stressful. Taking time for herself and resting during baby's resting time didn't seem so "wasteful" this time. Like so many other second-time-around mothers, Margaret learned to relax. She and Lew still made tape recordings of Patrick's baby babbling and then talking and singing, but instead of doing one of month, she made only three tapes during Patrick's first year and then a few more after that.

As the children grew, everyone in the Williams family found it relaxing to sit by the fireplace listening to tapes of old radio shows. Lew enjoyed throwing logs on the fire, and everyone would find a comfy spot for sitting or lying down. One cassette tape series became a family favorite—"The Cinnamon Bear," a holiday story that had originally been broadcast in the Midwest when Lew and Margaret were young children themselves.

Not everyone in the family shares the same sense of what's relaxing. Going for a drive, just looking around at the sights along the way, appeals to Margaret, but it sends Lew into "outer space." He never really enjoyed it as a child when his parents piled the boys into the car for a Sunday drive, whereas for Margaret it had been a weekly highlight of her early years.

Lew, on the other hand, is a lover of classical music. He can sit and listen for hours; after a short while Margaret will wander off, bored. She is a watcher, not a listener. She loves long walks, noticing details along the way, and she likes to record what she sees in her journal.

Old dog is one of my favorite neighborhood characters. He looks like a male lion these days because the fur on his rump and on his upper tail have pretty much disappeared, leaving a ruff of gray and black fur at his neck and a black tuft at the end of his tail. He has roamed this neighborhood for several years now, not really belonging to anyone, although he eats from a dish of food that gets left out at the tan stone house. He has no tags. He visits everybody's yards, just checking things out, barking a bit to let people know that he's there. He never growls and he seems to be rather good-natured, although he doesn't come around to get petted. Just an aged black spaniel who's had a hard life and has managed to avoid animal control for a long time.

Cynthia loves rigorous hikes in the mountains. As an eighth-grader, she chose to go to Yosemite and climb thousands of feet rather than take a plane to visit the attractions of Washington, D.C. For years, she loved running, and she loves to dance for fun, take walks, and work at jobs that have plenty of movement.

According to Patrick, however, you do not need to go tramping out in the country to find peace. Adding more work doesn't make sense to him, not if you are seeking tranquillity. He would rather sit in a big soft chair or propped up in bed just reading a book or spend time with a few friends.

Other families have different takes on parenting, Margaret notes. At a luncheon she once attended, one woman, an avid charity volunteer, described how she and her husband had been spoiling their two children.

"I guess we've been *overdoting*," she laughed. Everyone laughed with her, for they thought it was a good word, and they knew what she meant. As she described the things bought, sacrifices made, and behaviors condoned, it became apparent that the word was "too perfect." From purchasing the most perfect dog to creating the perfect Halloween costumes for her children, she and her husband had devoted their lives to the pursuit of perfect children.

Overdoting means that you talk about your children *a lot*. You talk about their clothes (Nike sneakers and special air features) and their toys (More software? Where will it all go?). You gossip about their schools (Why didn't they use the phonics series?) and camps (Space Camp is so educational!), as well as about religion (Their youth programs are so active!), and then you talk about the school employees (The Gifted and Talented teacher isn't the same as the last one) and about the principal (Well, she's at least better than the last one). Then you talk about the things you do for your children (four weeks to make a bear and a bunny costume) and the sacrifices you make for them (We chose the more expensive dog because a Dutch barge dog is *so* good with children). And, of course, you talk about their friends (His birthday was at the restaurant, all expense paid). Then you talk about rules (No Halloween candy until after breakfast) and about sports (soccer will never end). Finally, you talk about how hectic life is because of the *children*.

Margaret figured that the only antidote for an overdote was to go back to work.

A chipped cup retains its usefulness. Seek peace and quiet to set the world right. Set aside the moments you need for activities that will help you to center and find emotional tranquillity.

46. Be content with contentment

Wise parents learn that there are joys to be found in the simple pleasures of life. Friendships, reading, music, and enjoyment of nature can bring lifelong joy. Adventures need not be in expensive nor exotic places, for lavish desires may only create feelings of longing or jealousy. In the Way, parents also recognize that the warm, calm feelings of contentment are necessary for everyone in the family. Striving has its place, but not at the expense of mental and physical health. The peace of drifting off with the clouds during a restful time on the grass or of staring at a starry night sky can never be purchased. Ten extra minutes in bed or the afterglow of sitting by a warm fire can't be packaged.

Look for the pleasures that are simple to attain and easy to enjoy. Finding the basic aspects of life that give you pleasure is a task that will reward you and your family over and over again. Make a list and never forget.

Kate says that one of the happiest experiences in her life as a mom has been very simple. She will alway holds as special the memory of driving along in their car, on vacation, with her husband and children nestled around her sleeping in the quiet early morning light, drinking a good cup of black coffee as beautiful scenery slides by. Somehow, for her, the best moments in life have been associated with car travel throughout the western United States, because the family has had a chance to travel to Colorado many times in order to visit Carl's sister and brother-in-law.

Stopping for meals becomes a major event, punctuating the rolling passage of time and miles. Every person in the family gets a turn at choosing where to stop and eat. Breakfast at the Hungry Man Country Buffet or any comfortable local cafe is just great. The Flanagans are all fans of pancakes and hash browns. Lunch? Well, how about that fifties diner with jukeboxes at all the tables. Simply delicious hamburgers, and the rock-and-roll music MUST be played. Motown for Mom, please. Country road cafes and simple restaurants are the choice for dinner as well. No fast food when you're enjoying the countryside. And the motel? Well, any room with a clean window and a rollaway for whichever child whose turn it is will work just fine.

Vacation time at Aunt Barbara's and Uncle Jon's is spent doing a lot of visiting, doing a little bit of shopping, and taking a few hikes up into the Colorado mountains. The two families don't take any forced marches, for everyone enjoys the presence of nature all around, and strolling, not hiking, prevails. It is all right to stop to take in a view or enjoy the gentle coloring of a wildflower. Holly and Corey enjoy being with their three cousins, who are all girls and whose ages are in between Corey and Holly's. Aspen and pine boughs frame views of snow-capped mountains. Mountain streams roar and tumble over slippery rocks. The sky is wide and ever-changing, with shades of blue and gray and purple decorated by clouds of all sorts.

The best dinner of the week is always a barbecue picnic in the woods. Everyone helps pack up the bowls and containers in boxes, and off they go to one of several favorite spots that are close to home. Again, nothing fancy, but everyone is happy with Uncle Jon's juicy burgers on the outdoor grill and Aunt Barbara's traditional macaroni and potato salads.

Keeping things simple is pretty much the way with the Flanagans. Not that the children don't like to tease Carl about how *very* simple his tastes are. They like to say they are *too* simple! The clothes he wears come as gifts, for he never buys anything new for himself. "I already *have* a pair of pants, I *have* a shirt." And Carl doesn't need other things very often either. When he buys a new car every ten years or so, it is always one with no radio, and, as he puts it, "No nothing." He is very frugal for himself and doesn't feel the need to be lavished with gifts.

Carl simply teases other extended family members back when they ask why he and Kate live in their low-key neighborhood in a home that is very comfortable, but not fancy. "You know, I've been thinking about putting the washing machine out on the front porch so we can enjoy more fresh air when we do the clothes."

Spiritual, not material, contentment is true contentment.

47. Cultivate inner knowledge

Wise parents develop insight. They know that they do not have to go far to learn wisdom, and they know when to stay close to situations in order to clarify what's going on. People who become sensitive to others and learn to understand their children's motivations can be very powerful. They take care to question and think about the effects of their words and actions. They are also secure enough to ask for feedback from both children and fellow parents. They learn and grow from these responses.

Reflection does not require that you go any farther than your door. Learn to spend time thinking instead of "running around."

Often at the beginnings of the day Margaret writes in a journal. She writes in it for pleasure, but she also writes when something bothers her. At a back-to-school night, one teacher's talk really worried her.

She is a sparrow of a woman, boxy jacket hanging on a slight, short frame, hair pulled back in a George Washington ponytail that is brown and meager. She is proud of the schedule written in orderly white chalk. Every day has a purpose. Monday assign vocabulary words, Tuesday, grammar, handwriting, Wednesday vocabulary due, Thursday essays, Friday vocabulary test. It is the same every week. The books for the class have been selected for the students. The fall books are not as difficult to read as the spring books. For every book, there will be a test and there will be an essay. Each one has a specific number of points and every-thing will be divided with mathematical precision in order to calculate the students' grades. She understands that some of the students have already read *Macbeth*, but she hopes that they will forget it by spring because she loves the ghost.

She loves the ghost!

What about loving my child?!!!!!! And does my daughter care about the ghost?

Lew has a different schedule for his written reflections. He writes poems and fishing stories whenever he flies on an airplane. The ending of one poem talks about his favorite pastime.

Being a fisherman,
part of the fishes' world
and part of your own.

Maybe the fish
bring you closer to yourself
down deep.

Cynthia writes in her journal in phases. Sometimes she writes daily, and then periods will go by with no journaling at all. Her writing has been with her for a long time, though, thanks to several influential elementary teachers who encouraged her to keep a journal. When Cynthia was thirteen, her grandmother died, and she lost the person who had spent many after-school hours with her. She wrote about it.

> At the funeral home, sitting in the same room with her corpse in a wood and brass coffin with satin lining, made me realize she did quite a lot for me. Her watery cornflower blue eyes and rosy cheeks with delicate soft skin were some of her most memorable physical qualities. She was cheerful, with a good sense of humor, making everyone's spirits rise in some ways. Greatly will she be missed, for I have seen the grief of the people she brought happiness to.

Patrick, on the other hand, writes off and on in special-purpose journals, including a journal from school of his trip to Washington, D.C., and two other vacation journals. After visiting the Holocaust Museum with his eighth-grade class, he wrote about the experience.

> Instead of turning away, I looked closer. I felt like a clod. I was sad, but not that much. One of my good friends, Sandra Long, cried. Some people cried and/or were depressed. I know it doesn't seem right for me to take it differently between sexes, but I thought that it was funny for Eddie Smith to be bawling and hugging Mrs. Nelson, my geometry teacher. What's wrong with guys being as sensitive as some girls? I don't know, but I still felt that crying was wussy. I feel like a jerk saying that, though.

Regular self-reflection, if only for a few minutes, helps one to know oneself. It helps people know who they are, and who they once were.

The farther one travels, the less one knows.

48. The pursuit of the Way is effortless

Unlike the pursuit of learning, in which knowledge and skills can increase with effort day by day, growing in the Tao means decreased effort. The wise parent learns to work in effortless ways, doing things that come without stress. At the end of a good day he or she will say something like: "I don't know. Everything just seemed to flow."

Parent by doing what comes naturally to you. Remember that one family's dream may be another family's nightmare. If you wish to change your ways, make sure that the "fit" remains and that all family members benefit. They will let you know.

Dot and John have a deep commitment to their children and to their home, even though they both have busy careers. Sometimes work interferes with the smooth flow of home activities and responsibilities. As five children get older, their work schedules and school calendars add complex dimensions for coordination—nevertheless, the best times have always been when the whole family gets together.

Holidays "work" for the Singleton family, and the work to prepare meals becomes part of the enjoyment. Sibling rivalry is put aside, and events take on a pleasant glow. This blended family has been through a lot together. They all know that holidays aren't as much fun for some families but the Singleton gatherings are full of goofy fun, slapping good cheer, and flamboyant festivities. Everyone does what makes him or her comfortable.

Celebrations always mean lots and lots of food. A holiday breakfast will always have fruits—not just a couple, but eight to ten, and as many from the garden as possible, all sliced and cut in a colorful array thanks to Natalie and Dot. Everyone enjoys several kinds of breads with at least six kinds of cheese, with several coffee cakes and gooey pastries gathered from the local bakery in varieties designed to please everyone's tastes. John finds cooking a relaxing and enjoyable pastime. He cooks ham and eggs to order and flips pancakes to everyone's specifications. Ralph can pick up the guitar and get a medley of songs going that pleases everyone and gets several others singing.

Family "war stories" get retold and even seem to improve with age. Remember the time Mom stuck her head in the outhouse pit to rescue Ralph's new knife? Remember when the ball broke the plate glass window? Remember when Dad let us go off in the desert? Remember how we always went to the beach in our old green station wagon? Remember when we jumped off the roof into the pool? Remember when Polly lost her arches on our hiking trip? Remember the cabin in the desert? Remember when we invited the whole neighborhood over and Mom and Dad weren't home? Remember how we would slide down the mattresses? As the children turn thirty years old one by one, they have begun to take over the responsibilities of getting the clan together and preparing a holiday feast. As the words flow, tasks get done by someone in the seven-member family.

Grow by decreasing your efforts.

49. Regard children's ideas with respect and treat everyone with goodness and honesty

Wise parents learn not to be judgmental; they do not respond to their children by telling them they are wrong. They do not put down children, no matter who they are. Instead, they use words that can accept children's misguided ideas or inappropriate an-

swers and ask for the thinking behind them. They ask children to clarify opinions and facts. Wise parents are patient. Even a "smart remark" can be accepted and shown to be a useful remark—if only the context were different. In the Tao parents do, however, know to express displeasure if children transgress their own rules for fairness and politeness.

Learn to use children's ideas, for your acceptance will promote the risk-taking that allows them to become creative and critical thinkers.

In high school Samuel and Jacob were on the wrestling team and so were careful to watch what they ate. They got enough sleep. They tried to keep negative stress out of their lives. They also wanted to enjoy their years as high schoolers.

Since money was scarce at times, the boys thought up creative ideas for earning money here and there. Samuel had to pay for all his prom expenses. Tuxedos and flowers do not come cheaply, and he felt it was important that his date have not just a corsage, but a bouquet as well.

To pay for all of this, Samuel decided to participate in a contest that was similar to a beauty pageant, the Mister Savoy Contest. The newspaper announced the contest for the Saturday before the prom. It was being held nearby, just half an hour away at the beach. He signed up. But Mapita had misgivings. She felt that Miss America and Little Miss America contests exploited women and children and established narrow interpretations of beauty. At best, she had mixed emotions about his entering the contest, but he convinced her that there were no strings attached, no money to pay, and nothing at school that he would have to miss. He also assured her that he could handle the contest loss (or win) just fine. There would be several prizewinners, and any one of the several prizes would help him get to the prom and more.

Despite her misgivings, Mapita knew that Samuel had his heart set on entering the contest. She knew that he did not see anything wrong with his participation and she saw that, despite her feelings, she needed to respect her son's decision. He had been careful to select an opportunity that would be useful and would be fun. She did ask him how he could put himself on display and she was satisfied that he saw the event as an opportunity to teach others, as well as a chance to earn some money.

The contest turned out to need quite a bit of advance preparation. First he had to share a talent. Naturally, he thought of his wrestling ability, and he devised a skit with two friends dressed up as two typical teens, a girl and a boy walking down the sidewalk in jeans and shirts. They acted out getting into an argument with the boy starting to get rough and abusive. Along came Samuel to save the day—demonstrating and explaining the best and most effective holds. He took the bad guy down and walked off with the girl.

The next event was to be a skit about the contestant's future career. Samuel wanted to be a CIA agent some day, and he wrote a skit about being a spy. As he sat casually on a table, he received a phone call on a telephone embedded in his tennis shoe. He repeated out loud the exact details of his assignment, should he accept it, *Mission Impossible* style, including factual information about the responsibilities of an actual position with the CIA. In the next scene his ability to fight and defend the honor of his nation helped him vanquish a dangerous spy.

In the swimwear contest no skimpy suits were allowed; Samuel simply wore his conservative boxer-style blue trunks, which ended close to his knees, and a T-shirt.

For the question and answer session, which was to be handled in a business suit, Samuel wore his white shirt with suspenders instead of a suit jacket, partly because of his great love for suspenders and partly because he wasn't terribly excited about the jacket he was expected to wear.

The wrestling skit was well received, and everyone loved the telephone in the shoe. The question Samuel was asked to answer, handed to the emcee by a young woman who pulled it out of a special jar of question cards, was: "If you ever travel in a balloon, where would you like to land?" For Samuel, the answer was easy: "In Italy, the land of Romance."

When the winners were announced, Samuel's name was at the top. He had entertained the audience and informed the judges while teaching everyone some new ideas about wrestling. He proved himself to be a sincere and informative speaker. He knew how to hold the attention of a diverse group of people.

Mapita, whose emotional misgivings had stayed with her through the event, was satisfied that her son had maintained his dignity. The wrestling skills he had demonstrated were of a high level, and the humor and creativity that Samuel had shown were commendable. She was glad that he had participated and she was sure that the winners had been chosen fairly.

Make the minds of your children your own. The wise parent knows the needs of the child.

50. A person who does not strive intensely after life or tangle with danger can preserve life well

Juggling the responsibilities of maintaining a home, caring for children, and working are often compounded by other demands on parents—taking care of aging parents is one common experience. Wise parents choose their courses to fit their personalities. What may be too intense for one person can be a normal opportunity for another. The parent who suffers "burnout" is often one who did not know to choose personal priorities well. Rest, exercise, and reaching out to others are important for all. Nevertheless, danger does emerge for parents because of responsibilities that cannot go away.

Learn to relax from the tensions of your constant pressures as a parent. Use the Tao in situations of potential conflict.

For years, Margaret's neighbor, Myrna, has come by in the early hours each morning in order to walk up and down the hills of the neighborhood with her. Their main goal is exercise before they get involved with their busy work days. In addition, they share enjoyable conversation, corny little inside jokes that they have developed over the years, and appreciation of nature. Along the telephone wires above part of their route, crows love to congregate by the dozens and caw, bobbing up and down with the effort of their calls. The two walkers chuckle about the "party line" and walk on.

They also communicate during these times about family and neighborhood news. Margaret treasures finding out about school deadlines and notices that somehow have been overlooked or buried in the recesses of Patrick's school backpack. Reminding each other about which neighbors are coming or going on vacation is helpful too, to remember that the newspapers and mail need to be taken care of.

And meeting fellow walkers in the early morning light is always positive. Sometimes Margaret stops to chat. Whether it's a reminiscence about the great era of swing dancing, an insight from a recent trip to Colorado or Ensenada, a comment about viewing the comet, or sharing the pleasure of the jacaranda starting to bloom, the pleasantries are just that—a pleasant way to start the day.

Without these morning walks, Margaret knows that she would have missed the small things along the way. She wouldn't have known how gorgeous morning moons can be. She wouldn't have had the chance to see row upon row of bright pink and blue cloudbanks stretching across the eastern sky. She might have missed the mockingbird chasing the baby red-tailed hawk, and the red rooster crowing in the eucalyptus, and the owl hooting from the rooftop. She wouldn't have seen so many bright blossoms on the trees and flowers in bloom. But most of all, her days would not be as enjoyable without the treasured observations and comments shared between herself and her neighbor—two women who, with a laugh, call themselves the Neighborhood Watch.

In the Tao, subtle ways win. Cultivate life to avoid death.

51. Care for others without being possessive

Wise parents care greatly for their children, but they recognize clearly that those children do not belong to them.

Do not hesitate to get close to your children; allow them to know the various dimensions of your own humanity, and they will make their own choices.

John and Dot go out of their way to communicate with their kids. They believe their children need to be who they need to be, and that timelines are not the important thing. Going straight from high school to college for four years in a row may not be the thing for everyone.

Natalie decided that she needed to leave school to gain a better perspective on what her college education really meant. She became involved for four years with working on a cruise ship, and she will never forget those times. She held four different positions. One was as an art auction assistant, another was as crew store manager, the third was as cruise assistant, and the other was in costuming. In addition, she was, like all of the cruise staff, ready to fill in and help make sure that friendly, helpful service was always available on the ship. As Natalie put it, it was a time for "instant extroversion." Even though her jobs weren't terribly glamorous, she had a very exciting life. Wearing a formal four times a week, eating lobster, caviar, and other delicacies, and traveling to the Riviera, St. Petersburg, Bermuda, and European ports were basic parts of her new lifestyle. Getting acquainted with well-to-do and adventurous people helped her to expand her thinking about life. An eighty-year-old prince befriended her during one journey, and she was intrigued by his perspectives on social matters.

Natalie enjoyed this fast-paced life, but she knew that, in the end, she was who she was. She was still from her family's fold. Working hard for others less fortunate was important in the Singleton household. Natalie's social conscience ended up getting her back to school. Her decision.

Act beneficially, without the intent to control.

52. Enlightenment comes from valuing what is small

Wise parents do not ignore tiny incidents or occasions. They learn how to handle them or capitalize on them. From the child who has a small scratch to the one who has found a ladybug in the grass, all need to have your attention or a way to feel that they have your attention. Paying attention to things that may seem small reveals many of life's "teachable moments." Most important, parents in the Tao teach that they care.

Think about ways in which you can handle small things by giving responsibilities and outlets to your children. Family calendars are full of little events that can make a difference for you and your child if you attend. Recognize that many small things are important to children—and some can definitely "intrude" into your activities. Be there.

When Corey started to play football, he never complained to the coach. He never complained to his friends. But his parents heard a lot about each and every ache and pain after daily practices, especially during the first years. Kate and Carl knew that listening was probably a good thing to do. The bruises were real, and sometimes "letting it all hang out at home" helped heal things rapidly. Sitting on the couch with Corey, Kate liked to give him a back rub and hear how grueling the practice was. She knew also through patient listening she might hear any concerns beyond those that simply warranted friendly commiseration. The Flanagans had heard stories about football teams in other places where coaches really did expect too much of the kids and were abusive. They would have felt it necessary to step in if the coaches went too far.

Kate loved to attend the kids' games in various sports and going to a variety of events at school. In addition to being regular football game attendees, Carl and Kate spent many Saturdays together over the years, usually settled in matching blue beach chairs, watching soccer from the grass at the sidelines. They have always felt glad that they had their kids far enough apart so that they didn't have to race around, trying to cover two or three games in one day, the way many of their friends had to. Carl and Kate enjoyed these times away from phones and demands of work and home.

School conferences and plays also have always been important on the Flanagan calendar. Holly was unforgettable as a star in the second graders' version of *Nutcracker*. She was wearing thick glasses at the time, and she had a very "teacherly" quality; no one was surprised when she grabbed three little boys and nudged them off the stage when they missed their cue.

Conferences with the teachers were always informative, although Corey always thought that there were too many. Corey was not a rule-breaker, and he was always respectful to his teachers. He was definitely a good kid, but in third grade he began daydreaming, forgetting to do homework, and failing to listen when important things were said.

After one conference, Corey wrote a note that Kate and Carl tucked away in the scrapbook cabinet. They found it recently, and smiled at the big, round, manuscript printing.

Mom and Dad,
    Please don't kill me. I promise to get these grades: Math—A.
Religion—A. Reading—A. Science—A. Spelling—A. Again,
please don't get mad at me.

Love,
Corey

Corey had good intentions. And, as it turned out, his promise
was good—almost. At least he never again got the kind of grades
he earned in his worst daydreaming days.

Value small things. The Tao is in the details.

53. Do not indulge extravagant tastes; Do not indulge in excess; Do not get lost in solutions

*When life gets too full of busy-ness and material pursuits, pre-
dicaments arise. Wise parents know that problems have multiple
causes and that the web of factors can be overwhelming to deal
with. They do not, however, seek to deal with them all at once.
They recognize that reaching answers can only begin with one
small step. Then they choose the step and take it.*

*Do not choose elaborate plans when simple measures can
resolve some conditions or point out what other steps are appropriate. Things don't always need to go your way.*

An important rule at the Sanchez household is: "We don't sacri-
fice our health." With sons highly involved in school activities
each day and a single mother busy with her work responsibilities,
the Sanchez family needed to find ways to restore energy, deal
with chores, and enjoy their home. One simple solution seemed

to serve. Mapita and Jacob and Samuel agreed that one night, not two, was enough for entertainment each weekend. The fact that Mapita's sons only go out on one weekend night often seems rather strange to their friends, but it is a normal expectation and therefore, no big deal to Jacob and Samuel. Also, because their one-parent household has a limited economic base, some things were simply never issues for Mapita and the twins. At times, their "unusual" family practices have simply been the result of not enough money.

Still, one thing Mapita wished for her sons was to rent a limousine when they went to the prom their senior year. The boys had enjoyed attending dances all through high school and the limo idea seemed to be so wonderful. In her own mind, it was particularly appealing because she'd never had a chance to ride in one. It was associated with a lot of her own images of what was really special and elegant.

What she concluded, though, was "You can't give them everything." Because she had decided early on that schoolwork and school activities were top priorities, the boys did not have jobs outside of school. Plus, with all the expenses that pop up for seniors (various test fees, college application fees, graduation gown fees, prom expenses) the limo idea seemed to get buried.

The Sanchez family had one car and the boys had a system of taking turns. They counted on friends to deal with other needs for transportation, and prom night was no different. As things turned out, other friends who had rented a limo said that they wished they hadn't. For hundreds of additional dollars, they visited the same locales during the evening. They paid a great deal for the privilege of soft seats, great leg room, and being stared at for at least twenty seconds wherever they went.

It is often better to take city streets than travel the highway.

54. One who is established in the Way will persist and transform others

"Natural" parents are recognized by others, and their influence is great, not because of overt or powerful acts, but because of the ongoing lessons that their consistent behaviors provide. Much as rings surround movement in pools of still water, their affinity for parenting spreads to others around them.

Know that your parenting is appreciated by others. Do not think that because your acts seem small, your influence is not great.

When Mapita goes to wrestling meets, parents often come up to her. "You have such wonderful boys." "I want you to know that we feel we really can trust your boys." "They are such easy, sweet kids." "Those boys have such good manners." Mapita smiles and says, "Thank you." She knows, however, that she has not raised two perfect peas in a pod, but she is grateful that after many years of careful thinking and communicating with her boys, they are appreciated by others. She considers it very bad form to initiate any bragging about her two kids, so she does not chat about them at work unless her colleagues make inquiries. Instead, she realizes that people who spend time with her or the boys come to see how their way can work for them.

Mapita knows that she is not a perfect parent, but she frequently reflects about what has worked and what doesn't work in raising two active boys. She also rejects the harsh discipline that she had to endure as a girl. Her high expectations for the twins aren't just about manners. Their ideals reflect her own respect for all other people and her unwavering interest in promoting equality in society. She knows that her philosophy has always included a belief that her time with them was extremely important. Being present at home, attending the boys' activities, giving them many opportunities to know their extended family, and arranging a wide variety of real world experiences had made a difference. She knew that she wanted to make decisions that were consistent with her beliefs, and not only did she love her boys a great deal, she wanted them to know that her various decisions were made in a spirit of caring for their paths through life.

Whenever other adults get to know the Sanchez boys, they inevitably say something kind to Mapita. As one uncle put it, "They are genuine. Any time we get together at the house, they are really glad to see me. They aren't just buttering me up for something. Their manners and caring about other people aren't just for show. Mapita also knows that she can count on her boys to be helpful. If a guest comes to the house and brings a little child into an adult situation, the boys will be glad to find an appropriate activity and spend time and attention on the child. And it's not just in the family context that the boys have managed to develop genuine, positive relationships. Whether it is at church, at friends' homes, or in the homes of girls they are dating, the reaction is the same. The Sanchez boys are polite. They can be trusted.

When Jacob and Samuel were dating two girls at the end of their senior year of high school, the parents each mentioned that they relaxed when they knew their daughter's date was a Sanchez boy.

Cultivate the Tao in others by reflecting upon the things that you care about.

55. Stay in harmony by being in touch both with reality and with your original nature

Wise parents consider both external factors and their intuition when problems arise. When one child with a reputation for

picking on others is accused, one more time, of picking on an
"always-innocent" sibling, the situation may immediately sug-
gest guilt. Parents can easily go along with guilt by reputation.
However, in the Tao, the parent respects his or her intuition, bas-
ing judgments on far more than reputation in the moment-to-
moment events of living together. It means taking the time to
think about things from a variety of perspectives.

Get close to your children, for in doing so you can also de-
velop intuition about them. It will guide you in situations where
your instincts about relationships should have power over mere
circumstantial evidence.

Over the years, one of the ways in which Jacob and Samuel communicate with Mapita is through little notes left on the refrigerator or on the kitchen table for each other. It has been nice to
write and not just talk to each other. Although some notes have
been purely to pass on information, others have provided an avenue for deeper communication about important issues.

The boys were seldom sheltered from new ideas or different
ways of thinking. When Laura, their close family friend, had a
nephew dying of AIDS, everyone took on the business of supporting Laura's family. The boys wrote to their mother, "You
should have told us sooner. We take our lives for granted. We
could have spent more time with Laura's nephew." Their reactions gave her more information about who her sons really were.

Mapita had a good friend that she had made through work
and she decided that it would be nice to have this man join her
family for Easter dinner. This particular friend was gay, and she
usually would have discussed the situation with her sons before
he came. Instead, she kept quiet. She knew, since the boys had
Juan, a visitor from Mexico, staying with them, that it was a bad
time to try to talk it over with the boys because she knew that
their visitor was prejudiced. His feelings would have made everyone uneasy, for he was the sort of person who chose to speak his
mind regardless of others' feelings. She felt good knowing that

her own sons would be accepting, kind, and more open-minded about the subject, and later, they were indeed.

Harmony brings constancy.

56. It is impossible, with a person who has gained harmony, to be indifferent or intimate, to harm him or benefit him, to disgrace him or honor him

Wise parents learn to be self-accepting and reflective. They are impervious to the critical reactions to their parenting that might arise in others who are not in the Tao.

As you grow to be your own best judge, the judgments of others will mean less and less. Criticisms, even compliments, will not be taken personally, and you will remain detached enough to maintain balance and evenhandedness with both fellow parents and children.

For Carl and Kate, the judgments of others around them were easier to avoid with Corey than with Holly, their firstborn. By the time their second child came around, the two had gained more confidence as parents. Friends' and relatives' comments or opinions had far less bearing on their parenting decisions because they became secure in their own values.

Carl and Kate learned to say no when no seemed to be the wisest answer. Boundaries became clearer. At the same time, they learned to live more comfortably with flexibility and to honor their children's choices in other ways. They wanted to find a balance— they didn't want to be too controlling or too permissive. Especially as Corey turned eighteen, it was important for him to be less dependent and able to make decisions on his own, even though he was still an inexperienced young person economically supported by his parents' pocketbooks.

Common sense answers came more easily when they heard Corey plead that all the other kids are going to do it. "It" was, in one instance, taking a day off school in a so-called "ditch day" for seniors. The school sent letters to all the families requesting that no parents write notes to excuse students, for there was no sanctioned day to ditch school. The Corey version was that *everyone's* parents were going to write notes, and he would be the *only* one at school, and it was going to be *very* embarrassing, and he would *never* live it down. His parents, on the other hand, took a "broken-record" approach. "We expect you to go to school. We will not write a note. Things will be fine." Some parents did write notes, and some kids did spend the day at the beach. But most of Corey's friends were, indeed, at school. The parents that Carl and Kate knew had insisted that their seniors attend school, and although the day at school wasn't particularly full of excitement, the faculty made efforts to provide activities that were off the beaten track, and everyone was fine in the end.

Corey also wanted to take an expensive trip to a resort city in Mexico at the end of the school year. Although several years earlier, Holly had mentioned the possibility of such a holiday, she had never given it more than a passing thought. Corey, however, was very interested in going on this jaunt. As his parents began to ask around, however, the "educational values" and "careful chaperoning" advertised by the travel organization gave way to past participants' tales of huge hotels, characterless beaches, and tourist restaurants taken over by alcohol-dazed American students. The enjoyment of authentic cultural events was overshadowed by accounts of drunk and sick teens who couldn't resist the attractions of the lower drinking ages and intensified peer pressures to toss down beers and tequilas and have brief flings. In addition, some less common, but still factual stories about dealing with a very different legal system were none too reassuring. What they called their parenting common sense prevailed, as Carl and Kate looked at the picture for the long run, including college costs, and at the more meaningful gifts and trips that could come Corey's way. The answer was no. Yes, you are now an adult, and no, we can't support this with our funding.

When Kate went with her son to the end-of-the-year Mother-Son brunch at the high school, she was interested in hearing the conversations of many family duos around her. Several moms were sitting close enough to chat, and they said that since their children were adults now, they would have to let them go on the trip if they really wanted to. Kate kept her mouth shut, except to say that Corey wasn't planning to go. She and Corey had a great time at the brunch, and she began to hear about the *other* post-graduation plans that were hatching in her son's mind.

When in the Tao, one is aware that those who talk don't necessarily know.

57. Succeed with encouragement, not prohibitions

Every restriction can be met with resistance. The Tao is not dependent on rules for success. Wise parents do not post a dozen rules, even when they have been formed in consultation with the children. Rather, they develop the most important concepts— only three or so—that might positively guide their family. Such principles as "We respect other people" or "We respect learning" have greater power than admonishments like "Don't take things that aren't yours" or "Don't talk with your mouth full." Positive precepts can always be true.

Do not allow rules to become a rambling list of don'ts. Children are quick to test the exceptions, and they expect consequences to be applied uniformly to all offenders. Positive rules motivate; negative ones produce hostility and resistance.

In many tales, the stepmother has a bad reputation. Cinderella's story is, of course, a classic example; in fact, in *Hansel and Gretel*, a mean mother in the early versions was altered and became a wicked stepmother. Real moms don't do such bad things, according to popular thought.

When the new Singleton family came together, Polly had difficulty relating to her new stepmother. She was not happy with having to deal with this strange adult, and she was angry at her own mom and dad for "doing what they did to her." There was a lot of conflict—episodes of disobedience, yelling and screaming, and cussing. "Please turn the stereo down" was a signal for Polly to turn it up full blast. "I am afraid of snakes," signaled to Polly to scare Dot with a snake that had been purchased by her birth mother. Ultimately, Dot and John sought family counseling to deal with the psychological warfare. Things didn't improve right away—the counselor left when his own stepfamily was breaking up! Polly moved in and out of the house, had encounters with the police, and even had a brief stay in jail for being in a car with people who were taking cocaine.

Through it all, Dot refused to withhold love and tried not to have any "sick" rules—in other words, rules too stringent to be reasonable. She was intent on building respect and dignity in a situation that was characterized by defiance and resistance. Expectations were better than restrictions, and Dot and John tried to be encouraging. When Polly was finally ready to find acceptance, her stepmother was there to give it, generously. It took a long time for this blended family to get along and become close.

The more restrictions people have, the more outlaws will emerge.

58. A wise person governs in nondiscriminative ways

Parents might be wise to examine an old maxim, Rules are made to be broken. Sometimes truly equal treatment results from what seem to be unequal interpretations of rules. Always look to the values that rules are intended to uphold. The expectation that every child must have the dishes done by seven or have homework done by ten may be unnecessary. Age and situation actually can make a difference. In getting to know children's rhythms and needs well, parents can come to know what contexts are tolerable, possible, and desirable. In knowing themselves well, parents can learn to accommodate different children.

Do not discriminate against some children by permitting rules to have only singular interpretations. Discrimination implies that there is a preference for some or a prejudice toward others. Only rules that involve safety require unilateral, unquestioned, uniform obedience.

Lew and Margaret are like all parents. They want their children to act responsibly, follow through, and do their part. Both Williams kids do laundry instead of dishes. They have chores that are done every day or every week, like pouring the milk for supper or getting the mail. They are expected to get enough sleep, but instead of following a strict bedtime rule, they are allowed to adjust to the events of the school week, weekend, or vacation. Lew and Margaret want their family members to get exercise and fresh air, but organized sports are what the kids "get" to do, not what they've "got" to do.

The Williams family wasn't ever going to have a set of explicit rules that could be posted on the wall very easily, but there were strong implicit standards embedded in their lives. A good education is to be treasured. Respect teachers, but know they are human and make plenty of mistakes. Getting enough rest is important. Appreciate your family. School attendance is important. We strive to have good nutrition. Respect your elders. Protecting the environment is our way. You get what you pay for. Everybody makes mistakes, but there are always consequences of some sort.

Que sera, sera. What will be, will be. Overbearing government makes for indifferent people. Let some things take care of themselves.

59. Be frugal and accumulate virtue

Parents who "collect virtues" keep track of the good things that occur. Children are so often known by the negative things they do that their virtues can be overlooked. Wise parents acknowledge when their children have done good things, not through tangible rewards, but through their words. They encourage children to notice the ways in which they show responsibility and kindness to others. Wise parents help children to look for, and make note of, acts of generosity and virtue found at school, in the community, in the newspaper. They know that one individual can make a difference.

Help your children to see what a good place your family is and the world can be. Collect anecdotes about acts and activities that demonstrate how they enact things that the family values. Turn off the TV.

Samuel likes to quote a speaker he once heard at his high school who said that it isn't the SATs that count in life; it's the DIDs. Indeed, he and his brother Jacob both have many responsibilities and enjoy doing many different things. Because both Samuel and Jacob have been involved as officers of several organizations, they spend long hours at school. Typically, they're at school from

6:00 A.M. until 6:00 P.M. They come home to finish homework, eat, sleep, and get ready to go back to school. Unless there is a match or a meeting of some sort, the rhythm is pretty well set.

Participation in many organizations has come easily to the Sanchez boys, and their biggest supporter is their mother. As she reminds them, they are both friendly and know how to listen. Their leadership skills have been recognized since early in their high school days. They earned their DID credentials over and over again, becoming captains, co-captains, kings, and board members.

Not that it was always easy. Mapita has had to encourage them when things don't go right. If she is asked how the boys are doing, she will tell about their hard work and patience. She will always take the time to go to their school if either boy needs her to put in a good word for him. She also knows that sometimes she should remain behind the scenes.

Samuel decided to join a group called the Movimiento Estudianti Chicano de Atzlan (MEChA), an organization with roots in other political student movements of the 1960s and early 1970s. The MEChA organization served to bring people together, promote pride, and help others to see Central and South American indigenous peoples' social issues from new perspectives. Samuel was very proud of his great-grandmother, who was a Zacatecas Indian in Central Mexico, and he was anxious to participate fully in this organization. He was, however, not always embraced. He may have been a descendant of the right group—the indigenous, dark-skinned Native Americans of this continent, but he did not fit the image that many held of who belonged in the organization. Because of his European father, Samuel had a more almond skin tone than other group members. Having had an Italian father left him with incomplete credentials.

Nevertheless, Samuel was with the group when they left school one afternoon in early November to join a much larger congregation at the university in the next city. The political outcry was against a measure on the ballot that seemed to be unfair and prejudicial to immigrants. The MEChA members carried signs and let their viewpoints be known. When they returned to school the next day, Saturday detentions were waiting for all of them, because they had walked out of the school without permission. Samuel felt the detentions were unfair, when two hundred fellow students had, only one week earlier, ditched school to answer a radio deejay's offer of free admission at the local amusement park if you came dressed in a Halloween costume. Those students had received no punishment for their unexcused absences.

Although Samuel didn't like getting detention, MEChA helped him learn firsthand about political action. When he talked to his school administrators he politely presented reasons for his sense of justice. The students' punishment was not lifted, but Mapita let Samuel know that his interest in the political cause was to be commended. She was proud of his interest in making a difference.

Notice children's good habits early, they will serve them for a lifetime.

60. A wise person will neither harm nor constantly interfere with others

It is said that ruling a large country is like cooking a small fish. Similar care must be shown in guiding a family full of diverse children. Heavy-handed treatment can destroy what is good and whole. Hurting others is not possible for wise parents. They find ways to make the offensive acts of children seem inoffensive. The child who decorates the hallway wall with crayon drawings can be shown a better place for creating pictures and reminded that drawing is good and wanting to have a pretty home is wanting exactly what everyone wants.

Always try to see your relationships as you would want to see the liquid in the glass—half full, not half empty.

Mapita often tries to put herself in the boys' shoes. They live in different times from those she grew up in. She never talked back to her parents. Not ever. What requires time and effort for her is dealing with sons who talk back. They are boys. They are the twenty-first century.

For several years, she felt that she could not give up the old ways. She recalls that she spanked the boys a number of times during their elementary school years, believing that when spanks were delivered as consequences and not as spontaneous punishment in anger, the message was important. She changed as the boys grew, and she questions whether she could do what she did if things happened all over again.

Instead, as the boys grew, Mapita believed that the best procedure was to have frequent communication, and that included asking important questions that needed answers. She knew that her own upbringing slanted her thinking about many daily events and decisions, so she tried to keep the long view in mind: What will this mean for the boys' lives, not just the current situation?

One day, when Mapita was at work, she kept thinking about her sons. A feeling kept nagging at Mapita that something wasn't well with Jacob. She finally picked up the phone and called the attendance clerk at the high school. "Hello, Mrs. Sanchez. Yes, Jacob is in school. No, he hasn't been in the office." Moments later, however, the clerk interjected. "Oops, hold a minute. Sorry, I didn't see the memos in the other stack. Jacob went home right before sixth period. He wasn't feeling well. We called his aunt, as you'd directed on the emergency card."

So Mapita called her sister who told her that Jacob had gone straight home to bed. Then the plot thickened, for when she called their home number, Jacob did not answer. Then she knew exactly where he'd be. She decided to call his friend's house. Jose had a beautiful cousin who was visiting. Sure enough, with one more call to Jose's house Mapita located her son. Needless to say, Jacob was shocked to hear from his mother so soon after leaving school.

"How did you know I was sick?"

"I just knew somehow."

"How did you know I was here?"

"That did not require a Ph.D. degree. If you really are sick, go home to bed. See you at seven." Jacob was sort of sick, but he had been more intent upon impressing a lovely girl than going home to rest. Mapita understood that much, for she had listened carefully to her boys' conversations that week and she tried to think as her son would. No harsh words were necessary. Jacob knew that his mother knew him well. He also understood, without any further words, that he must not do what he'd done again.

Do not spend all your time weeding.

61. In placing yourself low, you take over others

Honoring others, including children, and showing pleasure in their company are wise practices. It is part of the Way to develop an attitude of being still, willing to take a lower position. In the Tao, parents also show their children the pleasures of getting to know other people from various backgrounds. It may mean spending time in places or situations that are unusual. Some circumstances may even be awkward. Sometimes it means finding unconventional ways to get to know the children better—attending an event that is off the beaten track for a mother or father. There is much to be learned from entering others' worlds.

Do not hesitate to express your interest in getting to know others; you have much to learn from them.

Margaret loves the saying, Make new friends, but keep the old. One is silver, the other gold. She has always enjoyed learning about the customs and interests of people different from her. Getting to know other people is something Lew treasures too, even though they do it in different ways. "Really, the shoe salesman does not have to become your best friend," Cynthia would say to her mother after learning about the background of the young Japanese fellow who was helping them in the shoe department at the mall. "But why do we have to go to *this* supermarket?" Patrick would ask his mom after trudging up and down the aisles of a Mexican-American market that highlighted cactus fruits and beef tongue.

Whenever the kids saw their Aunt June, they later asked, "Why does she talk to strangers all the time? She is friendly with everyone. Why does she want to know so much about people all of the time? Why do she and Uncle Jim travel so much with their Friendship Force group? Don't they get tired?"

Or they'd ask Lew, "You are having your students over to the house *again*?" And he would remind them that these were individuals from many different parts of the world, and the more they could get to know them, the better they would understand lots of other things.

But getting to know gets to go in many other directions. "You know, Patrick, *The Simpsons* is a pretty good show after all. I don't really hate it. I think Marge is great," Margaret said one day. "Her hair may be tall, blue, and bouffant, but her head is in the right place. Look what you've made out of me: I still can't stand Bart—he drives me crazy—but I'm a *Simpsons* fan."

And after listening to reggae music with Cynthia, Lew agreed that it was really pretty good listening. It was good to appreciate songs that had words he could actually hear and understand . . . and could think about.

Be receptive to all that will flow your way.

62. The Tao never rejects a bad person

Wise parents believe there is no bad person, although there may certainly be one who has made poor decisions. Parents help children to see people in many different lights. They may help children see what alternative decisions a person might have made, or they share how appropriate decisions have already affected the lives of others. Sometimes the person who has been difficult for the parents is their own child. Sometimes it is someone else who is close to the family in some way. In the Tao, parents try to look at individuals with many eyes. They know that prejudice can cloud perception in dangerous ways. Memories of another individual who promoted negative feelings may cloud the true picture of the present person.

Accentuate the positive. Help eliminate the negative. All children are worth your effort. Some need affection and kindness when they seem to deserve it least.

Carl and Kate were concerned when they realized what Holly's friend, Anna, was like. She was considered to be a "pain" by nearly everyone who dealt with her—parents, teachers, and peers. She often dressed very provocatively in tight and low-cut clothing, and she seemed to have nothing but boys on her mind. "He is such a hunk. Did you see the way he looked at me? How do you think he looks in a bathing suit? I think he likes you. I bet he kisses great."

On one hand, Carl and Kate were concerned that Holly spent so much time with her. Yet, as they got to know Anna, they realized that her troubled home life left her with poor role models at home. Understanding all that, they let Holly pursue her friendship, and they kept their eye on the situation. They were concerned Anna might be a bad influence on Holly, and decided it was best to keep an eye on the two of them at their home as much as possible. Kate and Carl also knew that a child without much guidance at her own house would benefit from getting to know some other parents. They did their best not to put a label on this friend who looked so grown up. Holly decided to continue to be Anna's friend, and she helped Anna through some very difficult times.

Anna may have had a wild side, and she may have expressed it in other places, but she was a thoughtful, chatty, friendly person at the Flanagan house, where she was always welcome. Kate has always believed that, on an individual basis, people can deal with one another well. She reserves her judgment when it comes to groups of kids; she knows that peer pressure can cause teenagers to do inappropriate things in order to impress their friends.

A wise person abandons no one.

63. Deal with the big while it is still small

Before problems escalate, the involved people must attend to them—or make an appointment for discussion to be held in the near future. With few schools able to hire many counselors, children must have other adults with whom to relate and examine their options. Other children can help, too, with suggestions, advice, and comfort for one another.

Set aside a time each day during which you will be willing to listen to children's problems. Be knowledgeable enough to deter children's easy fibs and dangerous lies. Look ahead to see when times for decisions and the need for information are approaching. Expect the unexpected, and you will not be surprised by what happens each day.

Lew and Margaret enjoyed driving their car around town. The trips offered the opportunity to talk and enjoy the kids a bit. The car was a place where there was no phone or TV. No one else was there to interrupt a conversation. It was clearly a good time for listening, and although lectures were ruled out, both parents were not beyond sharing incidents, perhaps dropping a few "pearls of wisdom." "Yes, we do expect you to help look for your lost retainer. Mistakes have consequences. That's right, everyone does make mistakes. That's okay as long as you try not to make the same mistakes twice." "I'm proud that you want to handle this yourself." Car trips provided bits of time to communicate about things that might otherwise get overlooked. Margaret and Lew know that there is listening, and there is listening between the lines. Sometimes they hear something that simply goes right over their heads because they don't know enough about the kids or their social contexts to "get" what they are hearing.

Margaret always insists that the addresses and phone numbers of her children's friends are written down, and it wasn't until high school years that she relaxed her insistence on knowing all the parents of her kids' friends personally. Nevertheless, she still believed in paying short visits to the living rooms or doorways of the homes of her children's close friends. She and Lew try to invite parents in or chat at the windows of their cars when the other parents are doing the driving. They know that a great amount of understanding can come from a little bit of knowledge.

Treat everything as if it is difficult, and it will not be difficult. Be prepared. Attend to tasks before they grow to dimensions that are difficult to handle. Do things bit by bit.

64. Put things in order before disorder arises

Wise parents know that some things simply have to be put in order for the family to function well and for everyone to stay healthy and out of one another's hair. The complexities of sched- ules for a family with several children can be disconcerting, as school, church, athletic, and social activities all need to get on the calendar. The intricacies of running a household with the laun- dry, dishes, trash, and paperwork that emerge by the day and by the hour can be frustrating.

Remember that as a parent, you do not have to do all the work. Your responsibilities lie in helping family members see how to handle their own affairs and how to do tasks that will help the family as a whole.

The Singleton family loved to go camping. But there was never enough money to just go out and buy camping things, so a system of borrowing each other's clothes and sharing hand-me-downs was put in place early on. Cousins and friends left small items, and John and Dot borrowed larger things from the church, such as a family-sized tent. The kindnesses of others made their trips to the outdoors possible. On the trips, every family member had an obligation to share in the responsibilities. Dot was always in charge of food and paper goods, and John was always in charge of the tent and other camping equipment.

At home, each person took care of his or her own room, but the family took turns each night at dishwashing duties. The boys had two nights of cooking each week. One person would dust, one vacuum, one clean the bathroom, one sweep the patio, and one feed the dogs. When Irma cooked, everyone was grateful, for she was able to put together great recipes and concentrated on quality ingredients.

Irma also liked things to be clean and orderly, and Dot learned she could depend on her for advice about arranging files in the home file drawers.

The Singleton family's automobile trips together are opportu- nities to get their lives in order. It's fine tuning time. About once a month or so, they get in the car and drive to a distant spot, some- times as far as the next state. The situation gives them a chance to discuss family "stuff," their ongoing changes in activities, and gradually altering nuances in values. They talk about the little things that count, telling stories of little incidents that get overlooked in the bustling about of regular day-to-day living. Then they probe large issues that need solutions.

Dot enjoys this poem that her sister once gave her.

Take Time
Take time to think, it is the source of power.
Take time to play, it is the secret of perpetual youth.
Take time to read, it is the fountain of wisdom.
Take time to love and to be loved, it is a God-given privilege.
Take time to be friendly, it is the road to happiness.
Take time to laugh, it is the music of the soul.
Take time to give, it is too short a day to be selfish.
Take time to enjoy your family, they are the jewels of your life.
—Anonymous

Be cautious at the beginning and at the end of a new project. See things to completion.

65. Do not try to rule through cleverness

Even though most parents are quite capable of making reasonable choices and decisions for their families, wise parents seek to make shared decisions with their children. Making unilateral decisions, no matter how wise, may help the family in the short run but probably does little to help children grow in problem-solving and decision making.

Accepting that you don't know, that you are indeed a beginner in life, allows your children to be smart.

The wrestling coach at Samuel and Jacob's school was young. He was new. He was well-meaning. But he and Mapita didn't get along. To make matters worse, he had been an elementary student of hers many years before, although they had gotten along in those days. As an adult, however, he had become an unthinking, sports-obsessed kind of guy. Mapita believed that school came first and sports was a sideline, and to her mind, the coach seemed to believe that the rest of the high school revolved around his program. He didn't always communicate with the classroom teachers, which added more problems. Many times the boys would have to leave class early for wrestling events, but would find out later that the coach hadn't consulted the teachers about it.

Although Mapita had several conversations with the coach, she always ended up feeling frustrated. To his way of thinking, she was an overprotective mother who was interfering with his business. He seemed to insinuate that she allowed the boys to hide behind her skirt. That made her even angrier. He insisted that he wasn't putting too much pressure on the boys. No, they weren't being asked to lose too much weight. No, they weren't endangering their health.

As time went by, the boys taught Mapita that it was all right for her to let them handle things with their coach. As they reasoned, they were old enough to speak up for themselves, and the coach was not alone among the coaches in some of his thinking. Mapita found it hard to stay on the sidelines, but for the most part she avoided further face-to-face encounters, and she came to realize that her sons were, indeed, competent and assertive. As a parent, she was better off permitting the boys to keep the communication open, and although there were plenty of decisions and events in which her voice was indirectly heard, the boys were the ones to do the listening and interpreting. The boys dealt with their own problems. They learned to deal with things themselves better and better. It was better that way.

Wise parents do not show off their intelligence.

66. Do not be competitive; do not oppress

This idea appears again and again in the Tao Te Ching. *Its message is emphatic, yet it is difficult for many individuals to interpret in a Western context. It suggests not only that we not compete with other families but also that mothers and fathers need not compete with one another. Moms and dads are individuals with distinct personalities, habits, likes and dislikes. One may be an early riser, the other may like to sleep in. One may like to relax in front of the TV, the other may love to be active. One may like to eat out, the other may prefer home-cooked meals. In spite of their differences, they can find the ways to model accommodation and harmony.*

Do not compete against one another; work together.

Lew and Margaret grew up in situations that, to most observers, were very similar: same religion, same geographic region, same race, same type of student, same college, same level of education—even the same kind of family summer vacation. Before they had their two children, they got along rather well. Money was never a particular problem with two incomes and the two could adjust to one another's schedules on a daily basis. However, when children came, a variety of issues surrounding how to spend time and money arose. Differences between the two emerged slowly but surely over the years. Lew had been raised in a loosely structured family of boys with both the benefits and the responsibilities of independence. Margaret, on the other hand, was one of three daughters who were raised with a strong sense of family obligation, reaping benefits and responsibilities along the way. Paychecks, clocks, and calendars were handled very differently in their respective family homes. As their own children grew, Lew and Margaret drew upon their respective pasts to view situations and they came to realize that they had very different bases for much of their decision making.

Margaret and Lew would get caught in arguments about a variety of family-bound decisions from breakfast to bedtime. Some of the related comments and replies sounded like these: "I can't help it if I don't like oatmeal!" "Why can't you leave five minutes earlier and get him to school on time?" "Dinner's ready and where are you?" "I do not *want* to take a walk because I do not *like* walks." "Stop acting as if you're so perfect." "Who are you, the Kitchen King?" "Stop being such a tightwad." "Why did you buy that?" "Why *can't* we watch TV during dinner?" "Who says the children have to be in bed?" "Why don't you get more sleep?" The power struggles were not constant, but when they erupted, they made everyone tired and tense.

Something that happened along the way helped to put things back into perspective for the Williams family. One week in late summer, Lew and Margaret decided to drive to Yosemite National Park with their children. They had been there many times before their kids came along, backpacking at high altitudes, cross-country skiing, and camping at various times of the year, but it had been years since they'd been there. Previously, they had treasured the atmosphere and scenery of their favorite park, for even during some of the crowded times, they'd always found places to enjoy in relative solitude, giving them the opportunity to refresh their relationship, a busy working couple.

Cabin reservations were impossible to obtain at such late notice. Instead, they headed to an isolated first-come first-serve campground to the south, above the valley. They arrived late on a sunny Sunday afternoon and spent the rest of the daylight hours finding and clearing a site with no visible neighbors, pitching tents, laying out sleeping bags, preparing and eating dinner, and cleaning up for a game of Crazy Eights played by the light of a lantern in the deep darkness of the forest.

For the next two days, as they hiked and fished and cooked and enjoyed being out in nature, any differences drifted away and disappeared. They walked through tall trees, past bubbling springs and yellow meadows, and by clear rushing waterfalls. Except for one walk when a burro shoved Margaret off the trail, all went well. They all enjoyed hot cereal in the cool mornings and they caught trout from a cold lake and cooked them over the campfire at night. Everyone pitched in to cook part of the meal and do part of the cleaning up. They played a variety of games at their wooden picnic table each night, enjoying roasted marshmallows, jokes and songs.

Since their Yosemite adventure, camping and outdoor times have always brought about harmony for the Williams family. The petty politics that emerge from maintaining a house and getting through busy days fall away. It is truly good to get away. Not that bad habits and old griping don't creep back into some of their days. But when Lew and Margaret reflect on how they make such a good team in the great out-of-doors it becomes easier, somehow, to see the other person's point of view during the events of leading "civilized" lives.

If you don't compete, no one can compete with you. The more you give to others, the more you possess. Allow yourself to be last.

67. Have compassion, practice frugality, be willing to follow

Wise parents always risk caring for others, for kindness lights the way to friendship. It is always reaped when it is sowed. In the Way, mothers and fathers acknowledge that acceptance of simplicity is a rich treasure. Common sense about money along the way provides security and independence for parents as they reach their later years. Parents are also not interested in acting as leaders at all times, for humility is an important trait in all great people. The ways in which cooperation can build our world into a better place can be taught well in the home.

Share your love with your children. Disencumber yourself from rich tastes and boundary-free credit cards that only create problems. Rid yourself of the need to be in control of situations at all times. Let others—children and adults—share leadership with you.

Kate and Carl know that love is certainly a lot more than words. Facial expressions, voice tone, eyes, smiles, hugs, and gentle humor all add to relationships at home and away. Kate has always felt strongly that people need to be treated in even, kind ways, whatever their status. Because she works at a school, she is in contact with many kinds of public school employees. She believes that each of her colleagues is important, and she enjoys her interactions and friendships with them immensely. The school custodian is important. Her teacher's aide is important. The office clerk is important. Their school secretary is important. The crossing guard at the corner is important. And, yes, the school principal is important. It is always part of her day to greet coworkers and exchange pleasantries.

Some principles seem to have prevailed at home over the years: We don't give people labels. No ethnic jokes get told around here. We really do try to judge people by the content of their character. Please, no sarcasm. And we don't believe in embarrassing people. Whoever you are, wherever you are, you are another human being deserving the respect equal to any honored guest in our home.

Loving kids just because they are who they are is a commitment at home, and it certainly extends to Kate in her work with young children. She often relates stories at home about some of her "naughty" kindergartners at school. Somehow, those very children usually end up being very special, although Kate has great affection for all her students. She shares with her family the joy that those five-year-olds bring to her, with all their honesty and joy in discovering every aspect of life and the world.

Kate and Carl often ask their own children for advice. They respect their children's opinions on a range of things—starting, of course, with trying to make sense of articles and pictures they see in the newspaper about various aspects of modern culture. When the Sunday magazine section highlights a fashion, Kate will ask, "Do real people wear these kinds of things, or are they just for models?" When a musical group is highlighted in the calendar section of the paper, Carl will ask what the kids know about them. He knows that he certainly isn't up on the various performers and their music.

Carl and Kate also recall that parental minds can change on some things. Corey wanted a dog, and requested that the family get one whenever they'd see a cute one on their various travels around town. The answer was always no.

In third grade, Corey wrote a story about "his" dog as a class assignment.

> I love my dog. He is cute and I like to play with him. He has a house in the back yard. I feed him dog food every day. He is a very good dog.

Corey's third-grade teacher happened to see Kate and mentioned the story.

A puppy walked into Kate's classroom late the following week. The custodian at her school followed the usual process of holding the dog for a day and asking around the school neighborhood carefully about owners before calling the animal control officer. Nobody had called or contacted the school by the end of the day, so Kate told the custodian that she would take the little puppy home "just for the weekend . . . in case the real owners responded to the lost dog signs over the weekend."

It took one weekend for the puppy to capture everyone's hearts. Corey finally got his dog.

Speak from behind; it allows you to remain in front without blocking the view.

68. Your appearance or position does not reveal your strength

Wise parents steer the boat by using the rudder in the back; they do not need to be at the prow to influence the direction being taken. Setting things up according to children's wishes puts the parent in a position to coach and support from behind.

Serve your children's needs in order to lead them. Be where they need you to be, at the right time and in the right place. Watching for these ahead of time takes some of the pressure off, and parenting becomes easier.

Joe was a baseball fan when he was young. When he was in elementary school, he collected baseball cards. He had hundreds of them, organized neatly by teams in shoeboxes on his closet shelves. He had even inherited a signed Babe Ruth baseball. Many a time the family waited at the gateways of Angel or Dodger Stadium so players could give him their autographs.

As he grew up, he began to outgrow this hobby. He decided to sell his cards and put an ad in the local newspaper. Despite the fact that his mom and dad asked him to keep his collection together, an older gentleman came to the house one day and offered Joe $150 for much of his set. He sold his goods and valuable cards; Dot and John's attempts to persuade him otherwise were ineffective. Several years later, he said, "You should have stopped me. Just think how valuable those cards would be. We could have paid for college. I had *all* the best cards!!!" But Dot and John recall that he was adamant at the time about making this decision. They regret that the cards were sold, but they don't regret the lesson learned.

You do not need to be first.

69. Do not delight in confrontation

There is seldom a need to confront children directly, and seldom a need to lose one's temper. They are both choices. Wise parents seek indirect ways to solve problems.

When confrontation becomes mandatory, as in a case where a child denies doing something that you have witnessed, express your regret at the conflict. Use positive goal statements. Instead of "You are lying," say "Always speak the truth."

Jacob lost all car privileges for two weeks because he was not in by the family weeknight curfew one Wednesday evening. Verlinda, a new friend, needed his help with algebra, so he spent four hours at her house helping her. When he got home at ten to eleven, he was met with a frosty greeting and Mapita's brief recitation of the consequences of his action. Jacob, however, felt the punishment was unfair. "Why should I be punished? You tell us all the time to help others! I was tutoring Verlinda in Math. She only called me at six o'clock. I gave Samuel the address and phone number. It isn't my fault he didn't tell you, Mom. I *was* in by curfew. I was home *before* eleven. . . . What's that? I know. I know. Eight o'clock is weekday curfew because of wrestling. But why should I be punished? I was doing something good for someone. We are *supposed* to be helpful . . ."

Getting around the issue—or at least trying to—isn't rare. Out-and-out lies are a different matter. Over the years, Mapita has tried to hold to the belief that if you tell a lie but then tell the truth about it, or do something bad, "we'll deal with it," but one is always expected to tell the truth.

The boys felt it was silly to lie, because "Mom will find out anyway." When the boys did do something wrong and they told the truth, Mapita always tried to praise them for telling the truth, but it did not mean that there were no consequences for the original misdeed. Not at all. But instead of laying down harsh punishment, she always asked what natural punishment had already occurred ("I lost my best knife and I miss it"), and then she'd consult with the boys as to "what more should be done." (For being careless, you have to pay for a new one all by yourself.)

Delight in non-confrontation. Retreating is a way to advance.

70. Be forthright and plain

Some families accumulate many "toys," buying the newest and most powerful electronics, fancy cars, boats and jet skis, and large-screen TVs. Likewise, some pursue activities that are more for show than for lasting pleasure. Doing things for the express purpose of getting the attention and/or adulation of others can only create problems. In the Tao, families develop hobbies and interests that can become healthy, lifelong pleasures. Parents who flaunt their success or personal wealth can predict that setting themselves apart does not endear them to others. However, success in and of itself does not produce an insufficient person. When financial opportunity comes along, wise parents use it to acquire classic, long-lasting possessions.

Try to keep "down" with the Jonses. Value subtle activities and simple possessions.

At times, Lew and Margaret wondered if they were "depriving" their children by having no swimming pool, no fancy or expensive cars, and few fancy playtime possessions. For fifteen years, Lew drove a 1966 VW bug, and he sold it for the same price he had paid for it. The next family car was a practical station wagon—a pre-owned car purchased from a relative for its practicality, not its stylishness. The Williamses thought cars were just conveniences that got people from one place to another safely.

One day, a student of Lew's was teasing him about the fact that he always wore a lot of conservative brown clothes. His retort was that he figured as long as he lived in a brown house and drove a brown car and had brown hair and wore brown shoes, he might as well wear brown clothes.

Margaret was not partial to brown clothes, but she found that she was also rather conservative in her dress. She learned that she could wear some kinds of plain-colored clothes for years, changing their tone with various accessories that she substituted over time. Since she always managed to drip spaghetti sauce on the days she wore light-colored outfits, she became attracted to prints and tones that hid stains. Her taste in sports clothes leaned toward jeans and plain sandals or sneakers, with sleeves that could roll up and down and layers that could be added or removed depending on the weather.

For years, the events in Lew's and Margaret's lives seemed never to require fancy clothes. Dinner parties were often casual or required work clothes. Formal dress just wasn't part of their way of life, until one fateful invitation came their way. They were expected to attend a work-related banquet that was black tie . . . and the implication was that such formal dress was *not* optional. Renting a tuxedo was something relatively painless for Lew. He found a conservative style and rented the whole suit, with shirt and tie and shoes. That was that. On the other hand, the thought of buying a fancy dress for a single occasion bothered Margaret. She heard about a gown rental store, but after visiting the shop and squeezing into several different dresses that rented for more than the purchase price of anything in her wardrobe, she headed off to the discount department store at the strip mall. There was a super sale on sparkly dresses, most of which were very short and simply out of the question for over-forty Margaret, in her mind. Luckily, the rack had a few dressy two-piece outfits as well, so a short dress became a long dress when attached to the skirt of another outfit with a few snips and cuts and sweeps of the sewing needle. The purchase price for two dresses was one-third of the price of a rental gown. When all was done, and the elegant couple got ready to depart, the children took snapshots as though it were prom night. And Patrick added, "Good job, Mom."

Wear precious jade only under a coarse shirt. Be forthright and plain.

71. When you don't know, say so

Children respect the parent who admits she or he doesn't know. Wise parents are certainly not all-knowing. Providing insights, provoking children's thinking and questions, and supporting efforts to obtain information are important tasks in the Tao. It is better to know but think that one does not know than to not know but think that one does. When parents don't know how to accomplish things, they have to think backwards. What do I want the kids to do? What do they need to do before that? And what do they need before that?

You don't have to know everything. Help children to learn who can be called on to help out instead of parents all the time. Your children will learn from what you do know. The rest, you and they can figure out together.

When Holly was struggling with one of her introductory architecture classes at the university, Carl and Kate couldn't help her since she was far away and neither of them knew anything about architecture. In high school, Holly had been a successful student. Now that she was in a new situation and in the midst of so many sharp students, she felt unsure what to do. She didn't want to "bother" the professor, but as her distress grew, her mom and dad suggested that she help herself by consulting with someone else. After unsuccessfully trying to find a friend who knew the material, Holly realized that the best person to get her straightened out was going to be the professor.

Visiting a professor's office for the first time was intimidating. First of all, she wasn't sure she'd even find his office in the hallways of the old brick building. When she did, she wasn't sure he was there, since the large oak door was closed. How strange to hear the professor call out, "Come on in." The door seemed huge, and it felt awfully heavy to open. The book-lined shelves on all four walls made her feel inadequate. Luckily, Dr. Patterson was polite and kind. He put her at ease about coming, saying that Holly was now taking one of the hardest courses and that she was definitely not alone in needing help over the rough spots. He was not only helpful, but understanding. He told her that it was his job to explain things a different way, and he suggested the name of a student who did tutoring. Holly realized that would probably be a good idea, and she asked her parents to help pay for the twice-weekly sessions. Holly was able to get by that semester thanks to her tutor, a junior named Bonnie who made sure that Holly understood the material.

That introductory course was a huge barrier to cross over. From then on, she found the course work much more interesting, and she felt able to work things out on her own. Kate and Carl knew that the tutoring fee was money well spent, for they might very well have had a daughter change her major simply because the introductory architecture course was such a "bear."

Step back so that the children will learn.

72. Be gentle to gain authority

Parenting involves subtle leadership. Mothers and fathers often see their children engaged in misguided activities or caught in the clutches of mistaken notions. Instead of insisting that their children are wrong with "Don't do that!", wise parents give children long reins. Instead of constantly giving advice, they ask for advice from their children. What would they do if they were the parents? They allow them to solve their own problems when they can. They respect the frequent demands of busy lives inside school and do not schedule children into lessons and sports that take up too much time and energy on a daily basis. Opportunities to do nothing must be respected at times.

Coordinate with everyone's schedule so as not to create cumbersome—or impossible—loads.

Both Patrick and Cynthia wanted to take piano lessons by the time they were in third grade. Cynthia lasted three years, with a friendly, rigorous teacher who taught at her baby grand piano in an apartment near the school, but Cynthia simply did not make the time to practice with her busy schedule of scouts, school activities, and sports. Worse, she felt simply awful whenever a recital was coming up. "My hands get so sweaty that my fingers slip off the keys!"

Margaret remembered that as an eighth grader, she had bad stage fright too. She had begged her parents to let her transfer from her teacher to a different piano teacher, one her friend had gone to for years. What she hadn't realized was that the new teacher held recitals. She never told her own children this until later, but Margaret had avoided ever telling her own parents about the piano recitals. Somehow she'd managed to avoid the whole nasty business before quitting lessons entirely.

Patrick made his piano lesson exit after experiencing three teachers at a local music studio. Miss Linda was the first one. She was young, attractive, and gave rewards for doing mundane exercises. Patrick thought she was great, but his parents were unimpressed by the exercises and colorless songs. Miss Linda announced at one point that she would be gone for a month and the owner of the studio would be substituting for her. There was a big difference; it turned out not to be in the material, for the music book remained the same. Instead, Mrs. Peters was a more creative and enthusiastic teacher. She had been teaching for many, many years. She cared about the music and she cared about Patrick. She called forth his talent instead of pouring on awards and chatter. When Patrick expressed an interest in other music and mentioned that he had written a song, Mrs. Peters immediately agreed to in-corporate his interests into the weekly lesson. Mrs. Peters still taught the keyboard skills and fingerings. She still expected prac-tice, but she had expectations of a different order and the four weeks went by rapidly. As Margaret recollects, the piano sounds would float out of the living room through the screen door and drift out into the neighborhood. For a while he loved the piano.

When Miss Linda came back, Patrick went back to exercise-style lessons, liking the teacher and learning the music. Lew and Mar-garet decided that Patrick wasn't being challenged enough. Mrs. Pe-ters had too many permanent students to take on someone new, so Mr. Roberts became his teacher. He was a lot of fun, and he as-signed a lot of good songs including a Scott Joplin–style piece, but he was too hard for Patrick. He began to refuse to go to his lessons. Lew and Margaret realized (too late) that instead of stopping lessons entirely (which is what happened) the golden moments ac-tually could have been revived. Their reflections, long after piano lesson days, helped them to see that teachers make a difference, and finding the right match would have been very important.

Patrick enjoyed going to lessons, despite the routine skills learned from Miss Linda. He was learning and growing. In the meantime, he could have joined a waiting list for lessons with Mrs. Peters. Had they listened, Patrick's words, and then his mu-sic, had much to tell. If only Lew and Margaret had known to talk more with Patrick. Perhaps he could have continued with his lessons and developed a talent that, clearly, was within.

Hold self-respect by respecting others.

73. There is victory in noncompetition

Parenting is not a race. There are no trophies, except for the good feeling of having a child who is caring and capable in the end. The fastest child doesn't necessarily win, nor does the brightest.

When you are at ease with yourself, you will be more at ease with your role as a parent. You will learn to be at ease when you feel supported. Parents who talk with one another can support each other.

Mapita has known hundreds of children well during her years as a parent and teacher. And, in spite of the fact that parents compliment her sons to her frequently, she knows that parenting is a day-to-day enterprise and that the successes of one week may pale next to the disasters of the next. She has learned to be very empathetic, and she even took up the opportunity to serve as a workshop leader for parents in the neighborhood of the school where she works. It seemed that all the mothers and fathers were struggling with how to get kids to obey and do the "right" thing, and the Spanish-speaking parents also felt that they needed guidelines to deal with a school that had unfamiliar practices and homework.

During Mapita's first year leading the workshops, the total number of regular parent participants who graduated from them was seventy-one. There were forty-one mothers and thirty dads. Parents could come to sessions in English or in Spanish, during the day or at night. The Spanish-speaking groups were twice as large—perhaps because, as one English-speaking mom said, "We tend to think we know it all."

Themes of various meetings included how to get information about the school programs, how to conference with teachers and ask good questions, and how to judge the quality of school activities. At-home themes revolved around seeing how the home can work with the school to promote positive behavior, manners, ethics, and self-esteem according to acceptable principles. Parents learned about everything from hugs to head lice.

At these classes, probably the most surprising lessons, or at least the ones that drew the most comments and questions, fell into two categories, corresponding to the two main groups of parents involved.

English-speaking parents asked a lot about how to deal with teachers and administrators at the school. Not only were they unsure who to ask what, but they felt very uncomfortable and even often felt unwelcome at the school as well. They left the workshops with a sense of how to ask for a parent-teacher conference, how to feel confident that calling in the principal is sometimes necessary and that one has a right to request that if satisfactory information can't be obtained from the classroom teacher.

The Spanish-speaking parents asked more about how to deal with the older kids in their families. They saw that their twelve- and thirteen-year-olds were getting harder to deal with. It was bothering them to feel that they were starting to lose their children. The parenting classes reassured them that although children remain individuals, they go through distinct phases.

Discussions of various situations proved very helpful for everyone in both groups.

Have the courage not to dare.

74. Obey your instincts

Wise mothers and fathers do not hesitate to do the things that seem natural and question things that don't feel right, even if objective analysis or popular opinion says they must be fine. If their own childhoods had been positive, they know that it is wise to act upon their parental intuition. They always use discretion in following trends. They honor the laws of nature. They do not fear reprisals from social custom or authority. Growth and success follow when parental ideas and natural authority conform.

Listen to your heart when puzzles about parenting plague your mind.

Kate was working as a kindergarten teacher and Carl worked at a construction site when their second baby was born. For the first several years of his life, Corey stayed with his grandmother while his parents worked. As he approached school age, however, his parents decided that it would be good for him to socialize with other children. Their decision about where to go for a day care program seemed rather simple, for every day both Carl and Kate drove by a children's center that was only a block away.

The center was in a large, attractive old house that had once been an elegant home in the community. A side driveway that ran under a portico allowed for the safe dropoff and pickup of children. Shiny, colorful figures of storybook characters stood several feet tall on the front lawn. In the enclosed back yard, children could play on a variety of well-made swings, bars, and bouncing toys under which soft rubber pads could soften any falls. Everything at the nursery school was well-maintained and clean. Furthermore, the neighbors all repeated stories they'd heard about what a safe, clean, efficient place it was. The cost per day was low, and the staff-to-children ratio was also low. As the newspaper ads promoted, Storybook Land provided wonderful facilities at fair rates. Carl and Kate decided that they should try it.

They waited until summer to make the move because Kate knew that she would have several weeks off. Corey could go to the new nursery school three days a week while she worked at various tasks that had piled up at home during the hectic school year. He could get used to the new surroundings so that the transition would be gradual. The entrance procedures were very clear. Carl and Kate filled out the forms that asked for health information and appropriate phone numbers to call in case of emergency. Corey could still be in diapers.

On his first day at Storybook Land, Corey brought his own special quilt for nap time. His mom and dad assured him that he would have a wonderful time, and they departed quickly. When Kate came to pick up her son at the end of the day, he was smiling and the director told her that he had had a good day. Everything was fine. The next morning, however, Corey did not want to go to the nursery school. Kate figured that he missed being with her since she was on her summer vacation from school, but she knew that he would get over his hesitation as soon as he got involved with the children and the program, so off they went.

Corey's morning behavior didn't change, however. He stopped complaining, but his usual positive morning attitude was gone. Something simply was not right, and Kate didn't know what it could be as the second week began. Carl and Kate asked Corey if another child was being mean, or if he was afraid of something at the school. No, there weren't any problems. At the end of the second week, Kate decided to walk to Storybook Land and spend some time with Corey instead of quickly dropping him off. As they entered, they saw several children quietly at play and the director said, "Corey, come in and put your things in your cubby. Hello, Mrs. Flanagan. Can I help you?" Everyone was polite. Everything was organized. But that's all it was. There was no warm welcome. There was no, "My you look nice today," or "We have some wonderful things planned today." Corey wasn't made to feel special, and neither was she. Kate observed several activities that morning that were sound for very young children, and the children's needs for clean clothes and good food were well met. But she simply did not feel right about the atmosphere. The tone was formal and sterile.

During the next two weeks Corey continued to go to Storybook Land. But Kate did not stay home to organize closets and clean house the way she'd intended. Instead she conducted a careful search for a daycare that would meet Corey's needs. Nothing fancy. Shiny figures on the front lawn weren't necessary. The toys wouldn't have to be the most expensive. But appreciation and love, genuine compliments and caring would have to be there. And, before the next week was over, they had met Roberta. She took care of children in her remodeled home in a neighborhood that was several miles away, not far off the street that Kate drove to work each day. It was to Roberta's house that Corey went for the next four years, which gave him the very best of everything, and fully deserved Kate and Carl's trust.

Kate looks back at that summer with relief, knowing that they could have easily kept Corey at the nearby center, persuading him that it was good for him. But she is glad that she followed her feelings about his going there.

Do not fear going against the tides of popular perception.

75. Strive in moderation

Wise parents avoid heavy-handed interference in the lives of their children. They suggest with care and permit them to make more and more of their own choices as they grow. When parents push their children into too many activities and pursuits, the results can be disastrous for everyone. Instead of developing eager, well-rounded individuals, their actions can promote shallow participation, stress, and discontent. In addition, some parents are overanxious to have their kids grow up. Some push upon their children the trappings of older ones with ill effects. In the Tao, parents learn to enjoy children as children.

Allow time for reflection, support reasonable choices, and relax.

When Patrick entered his teen years, everyone thought that he would continue to play basketball and join the school team. He was tall and talented, but Patrick had different ideas. He went to tryouts on the first day and discovered that the coach ran drills that mandated military precision, forceful chanting and shouting, and running around the gym with his hands held high above his head. According to the coach, this sort of discipline was good for young men. According to Patrick, it was barbaric. It was fine for other kids if they liked that sort of thing. He wanted no part of it.

As time went on, Margaret and Lew often suggested that he get involved in various extracurricular activities. They pointed out the virtues of this outside class or that summer camp, the enjoyment of various kinds of lessons, and the joys of being in many school activities, including games and dances. But the answer was almost always no. Many times, Patrick reminded his parents to remember how it was when they were growing up. "You didn't have to do all these things when *you* were young," he would point out. "Kids should play after school and summer is for relaxing." He assured them that it was fine to do things with his friends on the weekend as long as his homework got done. "Don't worry about me. I like to be at home. I can practice my drawing. Video games won't rot my brain. I might even sit and read a book."

Unlike many of his friends, Patrick did not rush around to a variety of obligatory activities after school. He chose to take lessons in drawing and painting one afternoon each week, he joined one club that met once a month, and most days he walked the two miles home from school, got a snack, and chose from an assortment of things that he liked to do at home. He lifted weights in the garage. He shot baskets on the driveway. He watched amateur talent on a television show that was broadcast in Spanish. He did homework for his classes in Spanish, chemistry, English, health, and trigonometry. He sent money to an organization that purchased cows for groups that were learning about animal husbandry in West Africa. And, for hours, he drew cartoons at his drafting table, practicing facial expressions or body parts or poses or contortions. He even painted the seat of a stool with a giant cartoon face.

Margaret and Lew noticed that Patrick actually did read books from the bookshelf at home, some that they'd never tackled until college. His arms became strong and muscular. His Spanish grew competent and he truly enjoyed the language. His grades were excellent. And his ability to draw expressive cartoons landed him assignments for the school newspaper. Patrick did things, but he did them his way.

Value life by not striving.

76. Those who are flexible are superior

Things that are hard and brittle are "comrades of death." Things that are supple and pliant are "comrades of life." Rigidity invites resistance. Great strength resides in being able to bend. Wise parents recognize the difference between having to back off and never having rigid dictates in the first place. When a child is getting into a negative activity or behavior, parents can provide distractions to steer the child away from trouble. With young boys and girls, an interesting book or sight can be just the thing. With older children, the prospect of going somewhere different, enjoying a surprise, or sharing a moment of humor can deflect or deflate potentially negative occurrences.

Be gentle and supple in how you handle your children. Remember that all rules have exceptions, and often the exceptions contain the seeds of new learning.

"Just say yes," is a joke at the Flanagans. It is funny because of its connection to the "Just say no" craze, but it is also very true and meaningful for the family. Someone will often say, "Just go with the flow," at home. Kate reminds everyone in her family that kindergarten teachers are experts at flexibility. Things *always* come up. Somebody's father is at the door and needs to chat about his child before he rushes off to work. A little girl has wet her pants and is embarrassed. A boy has just thrown up and he feels sick. The chicken eggs are hatching. A ladybug is on the carpet. The milk just spilled all over the table. Why get upset?

It isn't that things are all free-flowing and "do what you want" at the Flanagans. Holly and Corey have curfews. At the Flanagan house, school nights are for school work, not going out just for fun. Rooms need to be cleaned by Friday each week. Twelve-thirty a.m. is the designated Cinderella hour on weekends.

After many sports events, Corey arrives home earlier than

curfew, well before midnight. Still, all kinds of events crop up in teens' lives, and Carl and Kate are careful to listen to reasonable requests for altered plans. The night the team won a key basket-ball game, Corey didn't come home until after one, and then he wanted to go out to an all-night coffee shop/restaurant in the next city to celebrate with friends. He did just that. When a good friend had a party, he asked Corey to stay and help after the party. He was allowed to stay until the not-so-wee hours of the morning and clean up. Special events like going to the prom meant not having to come home until three a.m.

Life is soft and supple; death is hard and stiff.

77. Excellence is its own reward

Many parents offer incentives and rewards for their children's achievements, using allowances and handouts as rewards and punishments. After all, the society around them is full of tro-phies, medals, certificates, and cash. These incentives are all ex-ternal, or extrinsic, to the individual. In the Tao, parents find ways to encourage internal, or intrinsic, motivation within their offspring. Humility is part of the Way, and shares credit among all those who work together.

Learn to recognize the activities that provide joy and involve-ment for your children and reflect back to them, through your comments and questions, how engaging and pleasurable such things are for their own sake. Remember that bragging detracts from achievement.

When Patrick was a preschooler, he loved to draw. He could sit at the kitchen table, creating one creature or scene after the other, for an hour or longer. Margaret and Lew liked to hear the stories behind the pictures; they would always reveal more. As he went through elementary school, Patrick became known as an artist at every grade level. His teachers were accepting people; they allowed him to draw on the edges of assignments when his writing tasks were done, and they encouraged him to draw in response to many of the open-ended social studies and science activities. When his work was entered in school art contests it would sometimes win, but not always. Just as often another student's work was awarded the blue ribbon. However, the winner would say things like, "But Patrick is the *real* artist around here," and being the artist was what really held meaning for him.

Prizes also don't always mean what we think. Cynthia was a good writer all through high school. She never seemed to earn top praise from her English teacher, however, so it was nice for her when she won an award for writing excellence from the school district—a panel of judges from several high schools declared her senior composition one of the top seven collected from the six high schools in the district. It was clear that she wrote well and with passion when she had a topic that tugged at her. Cynthia was also quite enthusiastic and capable when it came to science, and entered the science fairs in high school with confidence. It was gratifying to her, and to Lew and Margaret, that she won two corporate science prizes and the Sweepstakes prize during the county science fair that year.

In the long run, however, the awards didn't indicate that Cynthia was meant to be an English major or a science major in college. Cynthia enjoyed winning, but listening to music and enjoying the many different avenues of creative art were more important to her. Her good presentation skills, careful artwork, and close observations of things that interested her were the real predictors of time well-spent, and perhaps a career well-planned.

The one who deserves merit claims no credit. Excellence is reward in itself.

78. Be soft and weak and hard and strong

Wise parents learn to shape themselves to their context. They must cope with various symptoms of changing times. Their guidance comes through being themselves and showing their children how they respond to situations rather than telling them what to do.

When in Rome, do as the Romans do, but maintain your individual identity. Remember that your children's decisions belong to your children.

Dot knows that it is important to be compassionate and understanding. She has learned that sometimes revealing her own weakness can give her children permission to do the same. It is OK not to be perfect. Show lots of love. Employ consistency with each child as an individual, but you don't have to treat everyone the same. And whenever you say anything, follow through.

When Polly was given a clothing allowance in the fall, it was made clear that it would have to cover all her purchases until spring. One year she decided on a pair of boots. They were beautiful boots—so beautiful, in fact, that they would take all of her money, every cent of it, to buy. That didn't stop Polly, though. Seldom did things stand in her way. She seemed to make decisions with calm and ease. Although John and Dot were tempted to criticize the extravagant purchase, they only complimented her on the boots, commented on the value, and knew that she would have to find ways to deal with her empty pockets.

Although Polly was sometimes known for her "attitude" toward authority figures in her human relationships, she always had a kind heart for animals. One winter, she went to a local pet store to purchase two rabbits. "Both females," the salesperson had said with confidence. But soon the two bunnies began having offspring. Pat and Pam had to be renamed Pat and Pete, and

Polly worried that the rabbit family was not protected in the makeshift fenced area in the side of the yard. She did not want the rabbits left outside during the rainy season, so she rearranged her room so the rabbits could live near her closet in a "jump-proof" corral she'd devised. However, within one day the furry visitors figured out how to leap the wall and make themselves at home in the entire room. By the second day, the pungent smell of rabbit pellets began to drift throughout the entire house. As John tells it, he "prevailed," and he helped Polly relocate the bunnies back outside, but with an upgraded shelter. He knew that the rabbits were important to her and her kindness to the rabbits was important for them to see. As per her design, he helped her to create a new residence. There was new wire fencing, a drop-through screen floor, and a roof that even channeled the rain off. All was well.

One must accept responsibility in order to lead. Guide with a firm but loving hand.

79. Do not attend to others' mistakes

Wise parents look for their children's successes. They do not blame others for problems that beset themselves or their children. Causes lie within. They do not blame the children for things that they do not know. In reading the things that their children write or observing the things they do, such parents try to find qualities to compliment or ideas to agree with. They know that children, along with other people of all ages, do not respond well to criticism.

Try never to belittle children in public. Have the children learn to be self-reflective. Trust that they can come to know when they've done a good job, and likewise recognize when they haven't.

As a quiet woman devoted to peace, Mapita struggled for a long time with her sons' athletic choices. Wrestling seemed so dangerous. Although she went to match after match, she also stayed home from some of the important meets, simply because they would be painful for her to watch. Still, she did not nag the boys about their "nasty" sport. She did not criticize their aggressive moves and frightening holds.

They were aggressive, all right. They wanted to be formidable opponents and champions. At the same time, they were full of compassion and were known never to hurt anyone just for the sake of being mean.

One meet stands out for Mapita. Samuel had been doing an amazing job for his team. In one match, when he was winning by five points, he had performed a head and arm throw when he saw that he was choking his opponent by the neck. He could have just kept holding him, because it was legal, but instead he figured out another strategy; he changed the hold to let the other guy breathe. In the end, Samuel won by a fall. When the meet was over, the boy from Kelly High School came over to Samuel and thanked him. Samuel says he will never forget how the boy looked when he said, "Thanks for loosening up on my neck."

Mapita knows, when she works with the parenting class at her school, coteaching with the community liaison, that two of the most difficult lessons are the ones with the following homework assignments: Apologize to your child for something you said or did that was harmful instead of helpful to him or her, and compliment each child directly about some specific things that he or she did. In response to these lessons, she spent time reflecting on her own family life. Apologizing is hard to do, because parents easily slip into the frame of mind that, because they are parents, they must be right; and even if they do want to apologize, the appropriate words are very difficult to find. Mapita tries to use words like "I know I don't know everything. I don't like to make mistakes, but I do, just like many parents." She is most conscious about lapses into nagging and apologizes when she does catch herself.

Remembering to give compliments is hard to do on a regular basis, but Mapita tries as often as she can. She recalls that when Jacob lent someone a cable box, she complimented him for being generous to other people. She also passed on compliments to both boys for being good guests at a work-related casual dinner. Although children were welcome to the casual event, the twins ended up being the only guests under thirty. The boys sat at different tables, away from their mom, and away from each other, munching on barbecue fare. Many adults came by at work the next day to exclaim to Mapita about what pleasant conversationalists her sons were and what a pleasure it was to meet them and spend time with them.

Goodness is in harmony with kindness. Do not blame someone else.

80. Be content and find delight in your home

Wise parents make their homes desirable places to be. The basic elements that "make a house a home" aren't terribly unique. Every home has beds and tables and places to relax. Most homes in this era have TVs as well. Clearly, the costliness and amounts of these items vary from one family's place to another's. Parents in the Tao realize that other homes are not necessarily better; they are different, and the important part of really "making a house a home" is the feeling tone, not the actual objects. An old, inexpensive coffee table that can accept a few tired feet at the end of the day might be more delightful to some family members than a glossy designer piece that screams, "Keep off!"

Concentrate on function for your home furnishings and let the environment support self-expression for various members of the family.

The Williams family home has a lived-in look. It is not a sleek place, and it definitely is not fancy. Most people would say that it is practical and comfortable. Margaret sometimes says that their home is decorated in "early Salvation Army." The dining set, living room chairs, bedroom chairs, desks, lamps, and many kitchen appliances were purchased secondhand, many from Salvation Army shops. Although they were made long ago—for example, the 1948 waffle iron—they do the job and look fine.

The decor includes contributions from each family member. Various paintings done by the children are hung throughout the house, interspersed with snapshots and prints gathered on family vacations over the years. Family photos hang on several walls. In addition, Margaret likes to collect statues or carvings of birds or people—but nothing fancy. She loves folk art, and she has included the children's clothespin art and woodshop art as significant parts of both her statuary collections. She also displays the little plastic husband and wife from the top of her parents' twenty-fifth anniversary cake from 1958 and a small soap sculpture of a family that she ordered from UNICEF during their Year of the Family. Each of the children's bedrooms has a bulletin board for their favorite tokens and mementos. The family bulletin board is in the laundry room—full of sketches, interesting sayings, and reminders. The other family bulletin board is the refrigerator door, which displays photos sent by friends or relatives, any awards or certificates received, cartoons from the paper, and important phone messages.

Margaret was eyeing the 1970 couch recently, thinking that its one orange, green, and gold reupholstering job was getting to look pretty dreary after surviving recent years of boys' overnights, regular encounters with popcorn and chips, and a year with their new indoor cat. Lew reminded her that a nice, new couch wouldn't stand up to the typical, ongoing assaults of the teens unless everyone got uptight and started to live more formally around the couch; he also reminded her that they couldn't afford a new one. Feeling rather discouraged about the shabby couch, she sat down to page through a gift book that Cynthia had given her the Christmas before. It held a message, for its pages throughout showed the "new" decorator look, and all the couches had loose slipcovers tied on them. She remembered that she hadn't exactly enjoyed sewing slipcovers for two daybeds years ago, but she sure knew how to shop for a low-cost, store-bought version of the style before her. To her way of thinking, a sort of a tan, dirt-colored one would be just lovely.

Remember that your own home is comfortable. The grass is not always greener on the other side of the hill . . . or town. High ceilings add to the heating bill.

81. True words are not fancy; fancy words are not true. The more you do for others, the more you gain

Wise parenting does not require the fancy words of an academic expert. It does need work in order to work—many hours of it. Add plain talk and common sense and throw in a few ideas that aren't so common in order to create a path that is part of the Way.

Even very young children can discover that it is pleasurable to give to others. For some children, sharing toys is difficult. Although sharing every belonging is not mandated, nor is it wise, parents can guide the process with care and discuss expectations for sharing before a time of getting together with friends. Any treasured item that might easily be broken by a guest should be put away. Seeing how sharing can give pleasure to Mom and Dad or to older siblings is important.

Teach your children the joys of helping others. Use caution, however, lest the effort spent helping others becomes too time-consuming. Children don't see helping others as particularly positive if it robs them of time with their own parents.

Right out of high school, Holly had an opportunity to volunteer for Habitat for Humanity in Watts that summer. At the job site, she worked on the security force, checking bags and noticing who went in and out of the project. During her university years, she volunteered at an elementary school in a working-class neighborhood near her campus. Several days a week, after school, she went over to the school to work with a series of elementary-grade "buddies," enjoying books together, playing word games, and tutoring reading skills.

Corey got involved with Special Olympics during high school. When he was just a freshperson he was signed up to serve as a contestant's guide and was paired with a seventeen-year-old who was six feet six inches tall and a very good athlete. Although it was awkward for Corey to interact with someone who was older, he tried to think of things to say as he went around helping his designated athlete. At the next Special Olympics, the person Corey assisted was a forty-year-old man. Corey was glad that he'd already gotten over worrying about older partners.

Volunteerism has always been encouraged in the Flanagan family. In her graduation speech from high school—as the valedictorian—Holly talked about her dad with pride.

Soon the 1960s rolled around, the generation of our parents; the generation that imagined all the people sharing all the world. . . . In this light, in another home, my father grew up inundated with the ideas of his day as he was developing his own. His parents shared a different set of ideals with him which they had accumulated along their roads, including a stress on sensitivity to all humans and an appreciation for humor. So began his road less traveled, which led him to Vietnam as a nineteen-year-old boy.

When Carl served with the air force in Vietnam during the sixties, he was assigned to a desk job in Bein Hoa. The days were filled with routines, writing orders, and other assorted paperwork. On the weekends, he traveled to the orphanage at the edge of the city in order to donate his time and services. There, at the fenced-in Catholic compound, with quarters in a Quonset hut, he helped with a variety of chores, mostly cleaning and small fix-it jobs. As each mealtime approached, he helped set up the tables with metal plates and plastic cups, and afterward helped clean up, noticing that there were few scraps. Before he went each time, he would stop at the military PX to buy candy bars and gum for the children and cigarettes for the nuns and other grown-ups.

The children looked forward to his visits. Not only did Carl bring them goodies, but he would play games and offer them companionship, smiling and laughing with them as they played. Play was simple; lacking a common language, Carl and the children played a lot of catch with a rubber ball and did a lot of good-natured chasing around. The kids were called "throwaways" by some, for they were the mixed-race children of Vietnamese women and an assortment of military men of various racial backgrounds. Fortunately, adoptions did occur regularly. Carl and Kate wrote and called one another, for they had decided that it would be wonderful to adopt a child. When a baby girl came up for adoption, they began to fill out the many adoption papers.

However, in their anticipation, they didn't realize that another family had applied to adopt the same girl. In a short time she was adopted by the other couple.

Carl and Kate were extremely disappointed, but with all the events surrounding his discharge from the service, their attention eventually turned to other things. It wasn't long before Kate announced that she was pregnant. And, as they now know, Holly was on the way.

Fulfillment comes from giving to others. Share your smiles.

Epilogue.
A Bit of Historical and Philosophical Background

Almost twenty-five hundred years ago, during the Golden Age of ancient China, a sage named Lao-tzu is thought to have taught in the royal courts—a Chinese scholar at the Court of Chou during the sixth century B.C. Many stories about Lao-tzu say that he became fed up with the spoiled feudal princes he was supposed to inspire. They were more interested in sport and eating and drinking than in listening to words of wisdom. He rode off on a buffalo (or some say in an ox-drawn cart) into regions beyond the empire's borders. At the frontier, the pass-keeper urged him to leave a record of his wisdom before he traveled on into the mountains. And so, brushing his way through five thousand characters, Lao-tzu is said to have written the original eighty-one chapters of the *Tao Te Ching* ("The Scripture of the Way and Its Virtue" and "The Book of How Things Work" are just two translations). He left behind an instruction manual for individuals to learn how to be happy and wise. Because of the book's close association with this one individual, it is often simply called the *Lao-Tzu*, although most modern scholars say that the chapters are really collections of writings and sayings by various people over time, not the work of a single person.

Lao-tzu and Confucius were but two of the hundreds of wandering sages of the time, wise men who instructed feudal princes and dukes. Before their time were the *yin* and *yang* philosophers and the *I Ching* (*Book of Changes*), both of which influenced the philosophies of these two great teachers, who ended up being the figureheads of Taoism and Confucianism. In both, *yin* (earth) and *yang* (heaven) represent the intercourse of the fiery golden dragon and the shining silver dragon, the ancient concept of the interplay of dark and light, ever changing like cloud formations. All things carry *yin* and hold to *yang*; their blended influence brings harmony.

The *Tao Te Ching*, with concise suggestions for living, holds special appeal. Its philosophy is not dependent on belief in specific gods nor prophets. The Tao (the Way) stresses virtue and wisdom, and it does not seek prominence, wealth, or status. Individualism is its hallmark, but a wise individual is unassuming, simple, and artless, certainly not egotistical. One should be selfless and be austere in personal furnishings. Moderation means to transcend passion, not suppress it. Immortality is won by acquiring the wisdom of acceptance and taking what comes along, for in going along with things, an individual avoids becoming separated from them.

The concepts of *yin* and *yang*, and the *yin/yang* symbol, have come to represent the Tao. All things, events, and beings are vary*ing* and unequal combinations of *yin* and *yang* in unceasing motion without beginning or end.

One may see here both unity and interdependence, for *yin* and *yang* attract one another like magnets with positive and negative poles. The force of their attraction becomes greater as the distance between them becomes greater. *Yin* understanding and wisdom must be balanced with *yang* energy to realize those qualities. Intuition is to be balanced with reason. Patience is to be balanced with progressiveness. Kindness is to be balanced with the application of intelligence. There is always *yin* within *yang*, *yang* within *yin*. In addition, *yin* and *yang* are relative; something may be *yang* in one context and *yin* in another.

The Tao also involves an intense appreciation of nature. Taoist poetry expresses affinity with nature and the many contrasts to be found there. Bliss is not blazing, it is tranquil. The Way emphasizes stillness, never expressing anger or greed, and the metaphor of the valley, which is lower than others, represents this philosophy better than that of the mountaintop. Taoism also enjoys humor and poking fun at itself. Embracing yoga, philosophy, folklore, and the arts, Taoism can and has been applied in poetry, painting, dancing, and music. Its influence has been great over the centuries, and it is a key to understanding many phases of Chinese life, including religion, government, art, medicine, and even cooking. Taoist teachers are not well known, but that would be in keeping with the humility espoused by the philosophy; the pursuit of gain and fame is not considered a proper human course.

Today over eighteen thousand interpretations of the *Tao Te Ching* are extant, with more than sixty translations into English. In addition, dozens of authors have applied its meaning for various aspects of living over the years. Since Lao-tzu wrote his work in response to the spoiled behaviors he witnessed in the courts of China two thousand five hundred years ago, his work surely holds important messages for parents of all kinds at all levels.

YIN AND YANG

Parenting in the Tao will involve the dynamic interactions of forces that are opposite in many ways. The chart below helps to show what some of the differences are. There are times in which you will sound more yang than yin, and others in which you will need to be more yin than yang.

Yang . . . . Yin

Yang	Yin
Let me tell you how I . . . saute onions.	Show me how to . . .
You may not . . . drink and drive.	It's your decision to . . .
The guidelines are clear . . . for this college application process.	What would you do . . . ?
You will . . . go to school and be on time.	It's a good idea to . . .
I'll talk with the teacher to hear all sides.	Good luck when you . . .
I love you.	I love you.
In our family we have respect for education.	What do you believe . . . ?
Please listen to me.	I'm listening.
Trust me.	I trust you.

. . . . Let's decide together . . . .